CODING
FOR KIDS 8-16

A Fun and Interactive Introduction to
Computer Programming and App Development

MICHAEL A. CHAMPAGNE

Table of Contents

Part I

Getting Started with the World of Code

CHAPTER 1

Welcome to the Amazing World of Coding!

This chapter marks the beginning of an exciting journey into the realm of computer programming, often simply referred to as "coding." For young minds aged 8 to 16, the world of technology might seem like a magical place filled with sleek gadgets and captivating software. But behind every app you use, every game you play, and every website you visit lies a set of instructions, meticulously crafted using code. This chapter will demystify the concept of coding and illuminate why it's not just a valuable skill for the future, but also an incredibly engaging and creative endeavor right now.

1.1 What is Coding and Why is it Super Cool?

Imagine you have a very intelligent but somewhat literal friend – a computer. This friend can perform amazing tasks, from calculating complex equations in the blink of an eye to displaying vibrant animations and connecting you with people across the globe. However, this friend needs very specific and clear instructions to do anything. Coding, in its essence, is the art and science of communicating with computers using a language they understand. These languages, like English or French, have their own vocabulary (keywords) and grammar (syntax) that allow us to tell the computer exactly what we want it to do.

Think of it like writing a recipe for a delicious cake. The recipe lists each ingredient and provides a step-by-step guide on how to mix and bake them. Similarly, code provides a set of instructions for the computer to follow, whether it's to display text on a screen, respond to a button click, calculate a score in a game, or even control a robot.

But why is coding so super cool? Let's explore some compelling reasons:

- It empowers you to create: Instead of just being a consumer of technology, coding allows you to become a creator. You can build your own games, design your own apps, create interactive stories, and even automate everyday tasks. Imagine bringing your wildest digital ideas to life!
- It fosters problem-solving skills: Coding is fundamentally about breaking down complex problems into smaller, manageable steps. When you encounter a bug (an error in your code), you learn to think logically, analyze the issue, and systematically find a solution. This critical thinking and problem-solving ability is

invaluable in all aspects of life, not just in front of a computer.

- It enhances logical thinking: Coding requires you to think in a structured and logical way. You learn about sequences, conditions (if this, then that), and loops (do this repeatedly). These concepts help you develop a more organized and analytical approach to problem-solving and decision-making.
- It unlocks creativity and innovation: While coding involves logic, it's also a highly creative process. You have the freedom to design the functionality and appearance of your creations. It's like having a digital canvas where you can paint with instructions and bring your unique visions to fruition.
- It's a skill for the future: In our increasingly digital world, coding is becoming a fundamental skill, much like reading and writing. From healthcare to entertainment, from

transportation to education, technology powered by code is shaping our future. Learning to code now equips you with a valuable skill set that will open doors to exciting opportunities in various fields.

- It's like learning a secret language: Once you understand the basics of coding, you'll start to see the digital world in a new light. You'll gain an understanding of how the software and applications you use every day actually work. It's like learning a secret language that allows you to understand the inner workings of technology.

- It can be incredibly fun! As you start to build your own projects and see your code come to life, you'll experience a sense of accomplishment and excitement. The process of creating something functional and interactive can be deeply rewarding and enjoyable.

In essence, coding is not just about writing lines of text; it's about thinking creatively, solving problems logically, and building the digital world around us. It's a superpower that allows you to transform your ideas into reality.

1.2 Computers: Your New Best Friends

Throughout this book, we'll be working closely with computers. But what exactly is a computer, and why should you consider it your new best friend in this coding adventure?

At its core, a computer is an electronic device that can perform calculations and process information according to a set of instructions. These instructions are, of course, the code we'll be learning to write. Computers come in many shapes and sizes, from the powerful desktop machines in our homes and schools to the sleek laptops we carry around, the tablets we use for entertainment, and even the smartphones in our pockets. They are all essentially sophisticated tools that can execute code to perform a wide range of tasks.

Think of a computer as a highly efficient and obedient assistant. It can:

- Store information: Like a vast digital library, a computer can store enormous amounts of data, from documents and pictures to music and videos.
- Process information: It can manipulate and transform data according to the instructions it receives. This could involve performing calculations, sorting lists, or editing images.
- Communicate with the outside world: Through the internet and various connections, computers can send and receive information, connecting us with people and resources globally.

- Perform tasks automatically: Once given the correct instructions (code), a computer can perform repetitive or complex tasks without getting tired or making mistakes.

Why are computers your new best friends in the world of coding?

- They are the canvas for your creations: Just as a painter needs a canvas and brushes, a coder needs a computer to write and run their code. The computer is the platform where your digital ideas will come to life.
- They provide instant feedback: When you write code and run it on a computer, you get immediate feedback on whether your instructions are working as intended. If there's an error, the computer will often tell you, helping you learn and debug your code.
- They are incredibly versatile: With the right code, a computer can do almost

anything you can imagine. This versatility makes it an incredibly powerful tool for learning, creating, and exploring.

- They are patient and persistent: Unlike human friends who might get tired or frustrated, a computer will patiently execute your code, no matter how many times you run it or how many errors you make. This allows you to experiment and learn at your own pace.
- They connect you to a vast world of learning: The internet, accessible through computers, is a treasure trove of coding resources, tutorials, communities, and inspiration. You can learn from experts, collaborate with other coders, and find solutions to your coding challenges.

As you embark on this coding journey, remember that the computer is your partner. It's a powerful tool that will help you learn, create, and explore the exciting world of programming. By understanding how to communicate with it through code, you'll unlock its immense potential and transform it into a true ally in your creative endeavors. Get ready to forge a fantastic friendship with your computer – it's about to become your most helpful and obedient creative companion!

1.3 Different Ways to Code: A Sneak Peek

The world of coding is vast and constantly evolving. While the underlying principle of providing instructions to a computer remains the same, the tools and techniques used can vary significantly. Here's a glimpse into some of the different ways you might encounter coding:

- Visual Programming Languages: Imagine building with digital LEGO bricks! Visual programming languages use graphical blocks that you can drag and drop to create sequences of instructions.[1] Each block represents a specific command, and you connect them in a logical order to make things happen on the screen.[2] This is a fantastic way for beginners to grasp the fundamental concepts of programming logic without getting bogged down in complex typing and syntax. Platforms like Scratch are excellent examples of visual programming environments, allowing you to create interactive stories, games, and animations with ease.[3] This approach emphasizes the flow of logic and the relationships between different actions, making it highly intuitive for younger learners.[4]

- Text-Based Programming Languages: As you progress in your coding journey, you'll likely encounter text-based programming languages. These languages involve typing out instructions using a specific set of keywords, symbols, and grammatical rules (syntax).[5] While they might seem a bit more intimidating at first, they offer greater flexibility and power in creating more complex and sophisticated software. There are countless text-based languages, each with its own strengths and applications. Some popular examples include:

- Python: Known for its readability and versatility, Python is a great language for beginners to transition to after visual programming.[6] It's used in web development, data science, artificial intelligence, and much more.
- JavaScript: The language of the web! JavaScript is essential for creating interactive websites, adding dynamic elements, and building web applications.[7]

- ○ Java: A robust and widely used language, particularly in enterprise-level applications and Android mobile app development.[8]
- ○ C++: A powerful and efficient language often used for game development, system programming, and high-performance applications.

- Each text-based language has its own unique syntax and features, but the core programming concepts you learn in visual environments will often translate across them. Think of it like learning different dialects of the same fundamental language.

- Web Development: This area of coding focuses specifically on building websites and web applications that you access through a web browser. It typically involves a combination of different languages and technologies:

- HTML (HyperText Markup Language): The structural foundation of a webpage, defining the content and layout.[9]
- CSS (Cascading Style Sheets): Used to control the visual presentation of a webpage, including colors, fonts, and layout.[10]
- JavaScript: As mentioned earlier, this adds interactivity and dynamic behavior to websites.[11]

- Web development allows you to create everything from simple personal websites to complex e-commerce platforms and social media networks.
- Mobile App Development: This involves creating applications that run on mobile devices like smartphones and tablets. You can build apps for different operating systems, primarily iOS (Apple) and Android. This often involves using specific programming

languages and development tools tailored for each platform. For example, you might use Swift or Objective-C for iOS development and Java or Kotlin for Android development. However, there are also cross-platform frameworks that allow you to write code once and deploy it on multiple operating systems.[12]

- Game Development: This exciting field combines coding with creativity and design to build video games.[13] It often involves using specialized game engines (software frameworks that provide tools and features for game creation) and programming languages like C#, C++, or scripting languages specific to the engine. Game development encompasses various aspects, including character movement, game logic, artificial intelligence for non-player characters, and user interface design.[14]

- Data Science and Artificial Intelligence (AI): These rapidly growing fields utilize coding to analyze large datasets, identify patterns, and build intelligent systems that can learn and make predictions.[15] Languages like Python and R are heavily used in data science and AI, along with specialized libraries and frameworks.[16]

This is just a brief overview, and there are many other specialized areas within coding. The good news is that the fundamental concepts you'll learn in this book, particularly in the initial visual programming stages, will provide a solid foundation for exploring any of these paths in the future. Don't feel overwhelmed by the variety; think of it as a world of exciting possibilities waiting for you to discover your passion!

1.4 Setting Up Your Coding Adventure (Tools and Platforms)

Before you can start writing your first lines of code and building amazing creations, you'll need to set up your coding environment. This typically involves having access to specific tools and platforms on your computer or tablet. The exact setup will depend on the type of coding we'll be exploring, but here are some general concepts and examples you might encounter:

- Web Browsers: For many introductory coding activities, especially those involving visual programming languages like Scratch or web-based development environments, all you need is a modern web browser (like Google Chrome, Mozilla Firefox, Safari, or Microsoft Edge) and an internet connection. These platforms often run directly in your browser, eliminating the need for complex installations.

- Desktop Applications (Integrated Development Environments - IDEs): For more advanced text-based coding, you might use dedicated software applications called Integrated Development Environments (IDEs) or text editors with coding features. These provide a more structured environment for writing, running, and debugging your code. Examples include:
    - Thonny: A beginner-friendly Python IDE that is often recommended for educational purposes.[17]
    - IDLE: Another simple IDE that comes bundled with Python.
    - Visual Studio Code (VS Code): A popular and powerful (but still accessible) code editor that supports many programming languages.

- Sublime Text: A lightweight and customizable text editor favored by many developers.[18]

These IDEs often offer features like syntax highlighting (coloring your code to make it easier to read), code completion (suggesting code as you type), and debugging tools (to help you find and fix errors).[19]

- Online Coding Platforms: There are numerous websites and platforms that provide interactive coding environments directly in your browser.[20] These can be excellent for learning and experimenting without needing to install anything on your computer. Examples include:
  - Codecademy: Offers interactive courses in various programming languages.[21]
  - Khan Academy: Provides introductory programming tutorials, particularly in

JavaScript and ProcessingJS (a visual programming language based on Java).[22]
  - Repl.it: A versatile online IDE that supports many programming languages and allows for collaborative coding.[23]
- App Development Tools: If we venture into building mobile apps, you might use platforms like:
  - MIT App Inventor: A block-based visual programming environment specifically designed for creating Android apps.[24] It's incredibly intuitive and a great way to learn the fundamentals of app development.
  - Thunkable: Another popular drag-and-drop platform for building cross-platform mobile apps.[25]
  - Android Studio and Xcode: More professional-grade IDEs

used for developing native Android and iOS apps respectively, which involve more text-based coding.

As we progress through this book, we will guide you through the specific tools and platforms we'll be using and provide clear instructions on how to get started. The goal is to make the setup process as smooth and straightforward as possible so you can focus on the exciting part – learning to code! Don't worry if some of these terms seem unfamiliar right now; we'll break everything down step by step.

1.5 Staying Safe and Being a Responsible Digital Citizen

As you embark on your coding adventure and become more active in the digital world, it's crucial to understand the importance of online safety and responsible digital citizenship. Just like learning the rules of the road before driving a car, understanding how to navigate the online world safely and ethically is essential.

Staying Safe Online:

- Protect Your Personal Information: Be cautious about sharing personal details like your full name, address, phone number, email address, passwords, and school information online. Only share this information with trusted adults, like your parents or guardians, and on secure websites.
- Create Strong Passwords: Use a combination of uppercase and lowercase letters, numbers, and symbols for your passwords. Don't use easily guessable information like your birthday or pet's name. Keep your passwords private and don't share them with anyone except trusted adults.
- Be Aware of Online Scams and Phishing: Be wary of suspicious

emails, messages, or websites that ask for personal information or money. Don't click on unfamiliar links or download attachments from unknown sources. If something seems too good to be true, it probably is.

- Think Before You Click and Share: Once something is shared online, it can be difficult to take it back. Be mindful of the photos, videos, and messages you share, and consider how they might be perceived by others now and in the future.

- Know Who You're Talking To Online: Be cautious about interacting with strangers online. Not everyone is who they say they are. If someone makes you feel uncomfortable or asks for personal information, tell a trusted adult immediately.

- Protect Your Devices from Viruses and Malware: Use antivirus software and keep your operating system and applications up to date to protect your computer and personal information from harmful software.[26]

- Take Breaks from Screens: Spending too much time in front of a screen can be harmful to your eyes and overall well-being. Remember to take regular breaks, stretch, and engage in offline activities.

Being a Responsible Digital Citizen:

- Be Respectful Online: Treat others with kindness and respect in your online interactions, just as you would in person. Avoid cyberbullying, spreading rumors, or posting hurtful comments.
- Give Credit Where It's Due: When using someone else's code, images, or other content in your projects, always give proper credit to the creator. This is important for respecting intellectual property and fostering a culture of ethical sharing.

- Understand Copyright and Fair Use: Learn about copyright laws and how you can legally use online content. Be aware of what you can share and modify and what requires permission.
- Be Mindful of Your Digital Footprint: Everything you do online leaves a digital footprint. Be aware of the information you are sharing and how it might be perceived by others in the future.
- Use Technology for Good: Think about how you can use your coding skills and digital knowledge to create positive change, solve problems, and help others.
- Report Inappropriate Content or Behavior: If you encounter something online that makes you feel uncomfortable, unsafe, or is against the rules, report it to a trusted adult or the platform administrator.

Learning to code is an exciting journey, and being a responsible digital citizen is an integral part of that journey. By understanding and practicing online safety and ethical behavior, you can make the most of the digital world while protecting yourself and respecting others. As you develop your coding skills, remember that with great power comes great responsibility – use your abilities to create positive and meaningful experiences in the digital realm.

CHAPTER 2

Thinking Like a Computer: The Basics of Logic

Now that we've dipped our toes into the exciting world of coding and understood the importance of our digital partnership with computers, it's time to delve into the core of how computers actually "think." Unlike humans who can rely on intuition, emotions, and context, computers operate based purely on logic. They follow a precise set of rules and instructions to perform tasks.[1] This chapter will introduce you to the fundamental principles of computational thinking, focusing on how to structure your thoughts in a way that a computer can understand. We'll explore the concept of algorithms as step-by-step instructions and the crucial skill of breaking down complex problems into simpler, more manageable parts. Mastering these foundational concepts is key to becoming a proficient coder, as they form the bedrock of all programming endeavors.

2.1 What are Algorithms? Step-by-Step Instructions

At the heart of every computer program lies an algorithm. Simply put, an algorithm is a well-defined sequence of instructions designed to perform a specific task or solve a particular problem.[2] Think of it as a detailed recipe, a set of assembly instructions for a piece of furniture, or a route map to reach a destination. Each step in an algorithm must be clear, unambiguous, and executable by the computer.[3]

Key Characteristics of an Algorithm:

- Well-defined: Each step in the algorithm must be precisely stated and leave no room for ambiguity or interpretation.[4] A computer needs to know exactly what to do at each point.[5]

- Finite: An algorithm must eventually come to an end after a finite number of steps.[6] It shouldn't run indefinitely without achieving its intended outcome.
- Input: An algorithm may take some input, which is the data it needs to work with.[7] This could be numbers, text, images, or any other form of information.
- Output: An algorithm produces some output, which is the result of processing the input according to the instructions.[8] This could be a calculated value, a displayed image, a modified piece of text, or an action performed.
- Effective: Each step in the algorithm must be feasible and can be carried out by the computer using the available resources.[9]

Examples of Algorithms in Everyday Life:

Believe it or not, you encounter and use algorithms all the time, even without realizing it!

- Making a cup of tea:
    1. Boil water.
    2. Place a tea bag in a cup.
    3. Pour the boiled water into the cup.
    4. Let it steep for a few minutes.
    5. Remove the tea bag.
    6. Add milk and/or sugar if desired.
- Finding a specific page in a book:
    1. Open the book.
    2. Look at the page numbers.
    3. If the current page number is less than the desired page number, turn forward.
    4. If the current page number is greater than the desired page number, turn backward.
    5. If the current page number is equal to the desired page number, stop.

6. Repeat steps 3-5 until the desired page is found.
- Following a recipe to bake cookies: Each step in the recipe, from gathering ingredients to baking and cooling, forms an algorithm to produce cookies.

Algorithms in Coding:

In the world of coding, algorithms are the building blocks of programs.[10] When you write code, you are essentially translating your algorithm into a language that the computer can understand. Here are some simple examples of algorithms you might implement in code:

- Calculating the sum of two numbers:
  1. Get the first number (input).
  2. Get the second number (input).
  3. Add the first number and the second number.
  4. Display the result (output).
- Checking if a number is even or odd:

1. Get the number (input).
2. Divide the number by 2.
3. If the remainder is 0, the number is even.
4. If the remainder is not 0, the number is odd.
5. Display the result (output).

- Displaying a greeting message a certain number of times:
    1. Set a counter to 0.
    2. While the counter is less than the desired number of times: a. Display the greeting message. b. Increase the counter by 1.

Understanding algorithms is crucial because it allows you to think logically about how to solve problems using a computer. Before you even start writing code in a specific language, you'll often need to design the algorithm – the sequence of steps – required to achieve your goal.[11]

2.2 Breaking Down Problems: Making Things Easier

Often, the tasks we want a computer to perform can be quite complex. Imagine trying to build an entire video game or a sophisticated mobile app all at once! It would be overwhelming and incredibly difficult to manage. This is where the powerful technique of problem decomposition comes into play.

Breaking down problems means taking a large, complex problem and dividing it into smaller, more manageable sub-problems.[12] Each of these sub-problems is simpler to understand, design an algorithm for, and eventually code. Once you have solutions for all the smaller parts, you can combine them to solve the original, larger problem.

Why is breaking down problems so important in coding?

- Reduces Complexity: Dealing with a small, well-defined task is much easier than tackling a massive, intricate problem all at once. It reduces cognitive overload and makes the overall process less daunting.

- Facilitates Algorithm Design: It's often easier to come up with a sequence of steps (an algorithm) for a smaller, specific sub-problem. You can focus your thinking on a limited scope and develop a clear and effective solution.
- Enables Modularity and Reusability: When you break down a problem into smaller, independent parts, you can often create reusable blocks of code (like functions, which we'll learn about later).[13] These blocks can be used in different parts of your program or even in other projects, saving you time and effort.
- Simplifies Testing and Debugging: It's much easier to test and find errors (bugs) in a small piece of code that performs a specific task than in a large, interconnected program. You

can isolate issues more effectively and fix them more quickly.

- Promotes Collaboration: In larger coding projects, teams of developers often work on different parts of the problem simultaneously.[14] Breaking down the project into well-defined modules allows for efficient collaboration and parallel development.[15]

How to Break Down Problems:

There's no single "magic formula" for breaking down problems, but here are some helpful strategies:

- Identify the Main Goal: First, clearly understand what the overall objective is. What is the final outcome you want to achieve?
- Identify the Major Steps: Think about the main actions or stages involved in reaching the goal. These will become

the high-level components of your solution.

- Decompose Each Major Step: Take each major step and see if it can be further divided into smaller, more specific tasks.[16] Continue this process until you reach a level where each sub-problem is relatively simple to solve.
- Look for Dependencies: Consider if any sub-problems depend on the completion of other sub-problems. This will help you determine the order in which you need to address them.
- Think About Inputs and Outputs: For each sub-problem, identify what information it needs (input) and what it should produce (output). This helps define the boundaries and purpose of each part.

Example: Building a Simple Calculator

Let's say our goal is to build a simple calculator that can perform addition, subtraction, multiplication, and division. We can break this down as follows:

1. Main Goal: Create a simple calculator.
2. Major Steps:
   - Get the first number from the user.
   - Get the operation to perform (+, -, *, /) from the user.
   - Get the second number from the user.
   - Perform the calculation based on the chosen operation.
   - Display the result.
3. Decomposing Further (Example for "Perform the calculation"):
   - If the operation is "+", add the two numbers.
   - If the operation is "-", subtract the second number from the first.
   - If the operation is "*", multiply the two numbers.
   - If the operation is "/", divide the first number by the second (and

handle potential division by zero errors).

By breaking down the calculator into these smaller steps, it becomes much easier to think about the algorithm for each part and eventually write the corresponding code.

Mastering the ability to think like a computer involves learning to express your ideas as clear, step-by-step algorithms and developing the skill of breaking down complex problems into manageable chunks.[17] These are fundamental skills that will serve you well throughout your coding journey, no matter what programming languages or projects you pursue. As you practice these techniques, you'll become a more efficient, logical, and confident coder, capable of tackling increasingly challenging and exciting endeavors.

2.3 Sequencing: Doing Things in the Right Order

In the realm of algorithms and computer programs, sequencing is the most basic and fundamental control flow structure. It simply means executing instructions one after another, in the exact order they are written. Just like following the steps in a recipe sequentially ensures the final dish turns out correctly, the order of instructions in a program dictates the outcome.

Imagine giving instructions to a robot to make a sandwich. The sequence of your instructions is critical:

1. Get two slices of bread.
2. Open the jar of peanut butter.
3. Spread peanut butter on one slice of bread.
4. Open the jar of jelly.
5. Spread jelly on the other slice of bread.
6. Put the two slices of bread together.

If you changed the order, for example, by trying to spread peanut butter before getting the bread, the robot wouldn't be able to complete the task correctly. Similarly, in coding, the order in which you write your instructions matters immensely. The computer will execute them line by line, from top to bottom (in most cases), and the final result will depend on this precise order.

Sequencing in Code:

In programming languages, each line of code typically represents a single instruction.[2] The computer executes these instructions in the order they appear in your program.[3]

Python

```
# Example in Python
print("Starting the process...")    # First
instruction
name = "Alice"                       # Second
instruction
```

```python
print("Hello,", name)              # Third instruction
age = 10                           # Fourth instruction
print("You are", age, "years old.") # Fifth instruction
```

In this simple Python example, the computer will first print "Starting the process...", then assign the value "Alice" to the variable name, then print "Hello, Alice", and so on. The output will be exactly in this sequence because the instructions are executed sequentially.

Importance of Correct Sequencing:

- Logical Flow: Correct sequencing ensures that the program follows a logical flow to achieve the desired outcome. Steps that depend on previous steps must come after them.
- Data Manipulation: Often, one instruction will modify data that is used by a subsequent instruction. Incorrect sequencing can lead to

errors because the data might not be in the expected state when it's used.[4]

- Control of Actions: In programs that interact with the real world (e.g., controlling robots or hardware), the sequence of commands is crucial for the correct operation of the device.

While sequencing is straightforward, it forms the foundation upon which more complex control flow structures like conditional statements and loops are built. Without a clear understanding of how instructions are executed sequentially, grasping these more advanced concepts becomes significantly harder.

2.4 Decisions, Decisions! Introducing Conditional Logic (If-Then)

Life is full of choices, and so is coding! Conditional logic, often expressed using "if-then" statements (and variations like "if-else" and "if-elif-else"), allows your programs to make decisions and execute different blocks of code based on whether certain conditions are true or false.[5] This ability to make choices is what makes programs dynamic and responsive to different inputs and situations.

Think about a simple game where a player earns points. The game might have a rule like: "If the player's score is greater than 100, then display a 'Level Up!' message." This is a conditional statement. The action (displaying the message) only happens if a specific condition (score > 100) is true.

The Basic "If" Statement:

The most fundamental conditional statement is the "if" statement.[6] It has the following structure:

If a certain condition is true, then perform a specific action (or a block of actions).

Example in Code (Python):

Python

```python
score = 75
if score > 100:
    print("Level Up!")  # This line will not be executed because the condition is false

score = 120
if score > 100:
    print("Level Up!")   # This line will be executed because the condition is true
```

"If-Else" Statement:

Often, you want to perform one action if a condition is true and a different action if it's false. This is where the "if-else" statement comes in:

If a certain condition is true, then perform action A.
Else (if the condition is false), then perform action B.

Example in Code (Python):

Python

```
age = 15
if age >= 16:
    print("You are eligible to drive.")
else:
    print("You are not yet eligible to drive.")
```

"If-Elif-Else" Statement:

Sometimes, you need to check multiple conditions in sequence. The "if-elif-else" statement allows you to do this:

If condition 1 is true, then perform action A.
Else if condition 2 is true, then perform action B.
Else (if none of the above conditions are true), then perform action C.

You can have multiple "elif" (else if) conditions to check various possibilities.

The first condition that evaluates to true will have its corresponding action executed, and the rest will be skipped.[7] The "else" block is executed only if none of the preceding "if" or "elif" conditions are true.[8]

Example in Code (Python):

Python

```
grade = 85
if grade >= 90:
    print("Excellent!")
elif grade >= 80:
    print("Very Good!")
elif grade >= 70:
    print("Good!")
else:
    print("Needs Improvement.")
```

Conditions:

The "certain condition" in an "if" statement is a logical expression that evaluates to either true or false. These conditions often involve comparisons using operators like:

- `>` (greater than)
- `<` (less than)
- `>=` (greater than or equal to)
- `<=` (less than or equal to)
- `==` (equal to)
- `!=` (not equal to)

You can also combine multiple conditions using logical operators like and (both conditions must be true), or (at least one condition must be true), and not (reverses the truth value of a condition).

Conditional logic is what gives programs the ability to respond intelligently to different situations and user inputs. It allows for branching execution paths, making programs more flexible and powerful.

2.5 Loops: Doing Things Again and Again (Repetition)

Imagine you need to print the numbers from 1 to 100. You could write 100 separate print() statements, but that would be tedious and inefficient. This is where loops come in handy. Loops are control flow structures that allow you to repeat a block of code multiple times, either a fixed number of times or until a certain condition is met.[9] This ability to automate repetitive tasks is one of the great strengths of computer programming.

There are two main types of loops commonly found in programming languages:

1. "For" Loops (Iteration):

"For" loops are typically used when you know in advance how many times you want to repeat a block of code.[10] They often iterate over a sequence of items, such as a list of numbers, a string of characters, or a range of values.

Example in Code (Python):

Python

```python
# Printing numbers from 1 to 5
for i in range(1, 6):
    print(i)


# Iterating through a list of fruits
fruits = ["apple", "banana", "cherry"]
for fruit in fruits:
    print("I like", fruit)
```

In the first example, the for loop iterates through the numbers generated by range(1, 6) (which includes 1, 2, 3, 4, and 5), and for each number, it executes the print(i) statement. In the second example, the loop iterates through each item in the fruits list, and for each fruit, it prints a message.

2. "While" Loops (Condition-Based Repetition):

"While" loops, on the other hand, continue to execute a block of code as long as a specified condition remains true. The loop will stop executing as soon as the condition becomes false.

Example in Code (Python):

Python

```
count = 0
while count < 5:
    print("Count is:", count)
    count = count + 1  # Important: This line ensures the condition will eventually become false
```

In this example, the while loop continues to print the value of count and increment it by 1 as long as count is less than 5. Once count reaches 5, the condition count < 5 becomes false, and the loop terminates.

Important Considerations with Loops:

- Infinite Loops: With "while" loops, it's crucial to ensure that the condition will eventually become false. If the condition never becomes false, the loop will run indefinitely, leading to an "infinite loop" which can cause your program to freeze or crash.[11]
- Loop Control Statements: Some programming languages provide statements like break (to exit a loop prematurely) and continue (to skip the current iteration and move to the next) to provide more control over loop execution.

Loops are incredibly powerful tools for automating repetitive tasks, processing large amounts of data, and creating dynamic and interactive programs.[12] Whether you're animating a character moving across the screen multiple times or processing a list of thousands of student grades, loops provide an efficient and concise way to handle repetition.[13]

Putting It All Together:

Sequencing, conditional logic, and loops are the fundamental building blocks of algorithmic thinking and computer programming.[14] By combining these three control flow structures, you can create programs that not only execute instructions in a specific order but also make decisions based on conditions and repeat actions as needed.[15] Mastering these concepts will empower you to design and build increasingly sophisticated and intelligent programs, bringing your creative ideas to life in the digital world. As you continue your coding journey, you'll see how these basic principles are applied and extended in countless ways to create the amazing technology we use every day.

CHAPTER 3

Visual Programming: Making Magic with Blocks

Having laid the groundwork for understanding the logical thinking behind coding, we now step into a realm that makes the initial learning process incredibly engaging and accessible: Visual Programming. Forget about complex syntax and endless lines of text for a moment. Visual programming offers a more intuitive and playful approach, allowing you to build programs by manipulating graphical blocks.[1]

It's like constructing with digital LEGO bricks, where each block represents a specific command or action. This chapter will introduce you to the exciting world of visual programming and guide you through exploring a popular visual programming environment, such as Scratch, highlighting its features and the fundamental coding concepts it beautifully illustrates.

3.1 What is Visual Programming? Drag and Drop Fun!

Visual programming languages (VPLs) represent a significant departure from traditional text-based coding.[2] Instead of typing out lines of code, you interact with a graphical user interface (GUI) where programming constructs are represented as visual blocks or icons.[3] These blocks can be dragged and dropped, connected to each other like puzzle pieces, to create sequences of instructions.[4] The shape, color, and labels on these blocks often provide visual cues about their function, making it easier to understand and assemble programs.[5]

The Core Idea: Abstraction and Intuition

The beauty of visual programming lies in its ability to abstract away the complexities of underlying code syntax. You don't need to worry about semicolons, specific keywords, or intricate grammar rules right away. Instead, you focus on the higher-level logic of your program. The visual nature of the blocks and their connections makes the flow of execution and the relationships between different commands more intuitive and easier to grasp, especially for beginners and younger learners.[6]

Key Advantages of Visual Programming:

- Lower Barrier to Entry: The drag-and-drop interface eliminates the initial hurdle of learning complex syntax, making coding accessible to a wider audience, including those who might find text-based coding intimidating at first.[7]
- Focus on Logic and Concepts: By abstracting away syntax, visual programming allows learners to concentrate on understanding fundamental programming concepts like sequencing, loops, conditional

statements, and events without getting bogged down in technical details.[8]

- Immediate Visual Feedback: As you assemble blocks, you often see the immediate results of your actions on the screen, whether it's a character moving, a sound playing, or an animation unfolding. This instant feedback loop makes learning more engaging and reinforces understanding.

- Encourages Experimentation and Creativity: The playful nature of dragging and dropping blocks encourages experimentation and allows you to quickly try out different ideas and see what happens.[9] This fosters creativity and a more exploratory approach to learning.

- Develops Foundational Programming Skills: Despite the visual interface, visual programming environments introduce core programming concepts that are transferable to text-based languages later on.[10] You learn about algorithms, logic, and problem-solving in a more engaging and less intimidating way.

- Ideal for Interactive Projects: Visual programming tools are particularly well-suited for creating interactive stories, animations, games, and simulations, making learning fun and relevant to the interests of many young learners.

Examples of Visual Programming Languages and Environments:

While we'll focus on Scratch in the next section, it's worth noting that other visual programming tools exist, each with its own strengths and target audience:

- Blockly: A library developed by Google that provides a visual block-based coding interface that can be embedded in web applications.[11] It's used in various educational platforms and tools.

- App Inventor: A web-based platform for building Android mobile applications using a block-based interface.[12]
- Snap!: An extension of Scratch developed at UC Berkeley, offering more advanced features and concepts while retaining the visual block-based approach.
- Tynker: Another popular platform for teaching coding to kids, offering a range of visual programming activities and courses.[13]

These tools demonstrate the versatility and power of visual programming in making coding accessible and enjoyable for learners of all ages.

3.2 Exploring a Visual Programming Environment (e.g., Scratch)

One of the most popular and widely used visual programming environments, especially for introducing coding to children and young adults, is Scratch.[14] Developed by the Lifelong Kindergarten group at the MIT Media Lab, Scratch provides a vibrant and interactive platform where you can create your own stories, games, and animations by snapping together colorful code blocks.[15]

Getting Started with Scratch:

Scratch is primarily a web-based platform, meaning you can access it through your web browser (though an offline editor is also available).[16] When you visit the Scratch website (scratch.mit.edu), you'll encounter a user-friendly interface divided into several key areas:

- The Stage: This is where your projects come to life! You'll see your characters (called "sprites"), backgrounds, and the visual output of your code displayed here.

- The Sprite Pane: This area lists all the sprites in your project. You can select a sprite to add code to it, change its appearance (costumes), or add sounds.
- The Blocks Palette: This is where the magic happens! The blocks palette is organized into different categories (Motion, Looks, Sound, Events, Control, Sensing, Operators, Variables, My Blocks), each containing blocks that perform specific actions.[17]
- The Code Area (Scripts Area): This is the central workspace where you drag blocks from the palette and connect them together in a logical sequence to create scripts for your sprites.[18]

Key Block Categories and Fundamental Concepts in Scratch:

As you explore the Blocks Palette, you'll encounter blocks that represent the core programming concepts we discussed in the previous chapter:

- Motion: These blocks control the movement and positioning of sprites on the Stage (e.g., move 10 steps, turn [clockwise v] 15 degrees, go to x: 0 y: 0). This demonstrates the concept of sequencing as you chain movement blocks together.
- Looks: These blocks control the appearance of sprites, such as changing their costume, size, showing or hiding them, and displaying speech bubbles or thoughts (e.g., say [Hello!] for 2 seconds, change costume to [costume1 v]).
- Sound: These blocks allow you to add and control sounds in your projects (e.g., play sound [Meow v] until done, change volume by 10).
- Events: These blocks define when certain actions should occur in your

program.[19] The most common starting block is when [green flag v] clicked, which triggers the connected script when the green flag above the Stage is clicked. Other event blocks respond to keyboard presses, mouse clicks, or messages broadcast by other sprites.[20] This introduces the concept of event-driven programming.

- Control: This category contains blocks that implement conditional logic (e.g., if <condition> then ..., if <condition> then ... else ...) and loops (e.g., repeat 10, forever, repeat until <condition>). These blocks allow your sprites to make decisions and perform actions repeatedly.

- Sensing: These blocks allow your sprites to interact with the environment and user input. They can detect things like touching other sprites, touching a specific color, the distance to another sprite, mouse position, and keyboard input (e.g., touching [mouse-pointer v] ?, key [space v] pressed ?).

- Operators: These blocks perform mathematical operations (addition, subtraction, multiplication, division), comparisons (>, <, =), and logical operations (and, or, not). They are often used within conditional and loop blocks to create more complex logic.
- Variables: This category allows you to create and manage variables, which are named storage locations that can hold values (numbers, text, etc.) that can change during the execution of your program. This is a fundamental concept for storing and manipulating data.
- My Blocks: This advanced feature allows you to define your own custom blocks, which can help organize your code and make it more reusable, introducing the concept of functions or procedures.[21]

Creating Your First Project in Scratch:

The best way to learn Scratch is by doing! You can start by exploring the interface, experimenting with dragging and dropping different blocks, and seeing what they do on the Stage. Many tutorials and starter projects are available on the Scratch website to guide you through the process of creating simple animations, interactive stories, and basic games.[22]

Example: Making a Cat Sprite Move and Say "Hello!"

1. Select the default cat sprite. It should already be on the Stage when you create a new project.
2. Go to the "Events" category in the Blocks Palette and drag the when [green flag v] clicked block to the Code Area. This tells the script to start running when you click the green flag.
3. Go to the "Motion" category and drag the move 10 steps block and attach it

below the "when green flag clicked" block.

4. Go to the "Looks" category and drag the say [Hello!] for 2 seconds block and attach it below the "move 10 steps" block.

Now, when you click the green flag above the Stage, the cat sprite will move a little and then say "Hello!" for two seconds. This simple example demonstrates the concept of sequencing.

You can then experiment with adding more blocks to make the cat move in different ways, turn, change its appearance, play sounds, and respond to user interaction.

Scratch as a Stepping Stone:

While Scratch provides a fun and accessible entry point to coding, it also lays a strong foundation for understanding more advanced programming concepts.[23] The logical structures you learn to build with blocks directly correspond to the control flow structures found in text-based languages. For example, the "if" block in Scratch functions similarly to the if statement in Python or JavaScript, and the "repeat" block is analogous to "for" loops.

By engaging with visual programming environments like Scratch, you'll develop crucial computational thinking skills, including problem-solving, logical reasoning, and creative expression, all while having fun and making your digital ideas come to life.[24] It's a fantastic way to build confidence and enthusiasm for the world of coding before venturing into the more textual realms. So, get ready to drag, drop, and discover the magic of visual programming!

3.3 Moving Characters and Objects

One of the first steps in making your visual programs engaging is to bring movement to your sprites. In Scratch (and other visual programming environments), there are various blocks within the Motion category that allow you to control the position and orientation of your characters and objects on the Stage. Understanding these blocks is key to creating dynamic games, animations, and interactive stories.

Basic Movement:

- move [ ] steps: This is the most fundamental movement block. It moves the selected sprite forward in its current direction by the specified number of steps.[1] A positive number moves it forward, while a negative number moves it backward. Experimenting with different step values will result in varying speeds and distances of movement.[2]

- turn [clockwise v] [ ] degrees and turn [counter-clockwise v] [ ] degrees: These blocks rotate the sprite by the specified number of degrees, either clockwise or counter-clockwise.[3] This is essential for changing the direction of movement or creating spinning effects.
- go to x: [ ] y: [ ]: This block instantly positions the sprite at the specified coordinates on the Stage.[4] The Stage has a central point at (0, 0), with x-coordinates ranging roughly from -240 to 240 (left to right) and y-coordinates from -180 to 180 (bottom to top). This is useful for placing sprites in specific locations or resetting their positions.
- go to [mouse-pointer v] or go to [random position v]: These blocks provide dynamic positioning. The sprite will either follow the mouse cursor or jump to a random location on the Stage. This can be used for

interactive elements or creating unpredictable movements.

Controlled and Continuous Movement:

To create more controlled and continuous movement, you often combine these basic motion blocks with other control flow structures:

- forever loop: Wrapping a move block inside a forever loop will make the sprite move continuously in its current direction. You'll often need to combine this with other blocks to prevent the sprite from moving off-screen (e.g., using the if on edge, bounce block).
- repeat [ ] loop: If you want a sprite to move a specific distance or perform a sequence of movements a certain number of times, you can use the repeat block.
- Conditional Movement with if statements: You can use sensing blocks (like key [ ] pressed?) within an if statement to make a sprite move

only when a specific key is pressed. This is fundamental for creating player-controlled characters in games.

Example: Making a Cat Walk Back and Forth:
1. Add a cat sprite to your project.
2. Create the following script for the cat:
3. Code snippet

```
when [green flag v] clicked
forever
    move 10 steps
    if on edge, bounce
    wait 1 seconds
```

   4.
5. This script will make the cat move 10 steps, bounce off the edge of the Stage if it reaches it, and then wait for 1 second before repeating the process.

Beyond Basic Movement:

As you become more comfortable, you can explore more advanced motion blocks like glide [ ] secs to x: [ ] y: [ ] which creates a smooth, animated movement to a specific coordinate over a set duration, and blocks that allow you to change the sprite's x and y coordinates directly (change x by [ ], change y by [ ]), providing finer control over movement, especially when combined with variables.

3.4 Making Things Interact: Events and Actions

Making your digital creations truly engaging involves creating interactions between different elements. This is where events and actions come into play. Events are occurrences that trigger specific actions within your program.[5] In Scratch, the Events category provides the blocks that define these triggers.[6]

Common Event Blocks:

- when [green flag v] clicked: As we've seen, this is the starting point for many scripts, initiating actions when the user clicks the green flag.
- when this sprite clicked: This event triggers the attached script when the user clicks on the specific sprite.[7] This is crucial for creating interactive buttons or elements that respond to direct user input.
- when key [ ] pressed: This event triggers the script when a specific key on the keyboard is pressed. This is fundamental for controlling characters in games or responding to keyboard input.
- when backdrop switches to [ ]: This event triggers when the background of the Stage changes. This can be used to coordinate actions with scene changes in a story or game.
- when [loudness v] > [ ]: This event can be used to make your program

respond to sound levels detected by the microphone.

- receive [message1 v] and broadcast [message1 v] / broadcast [message1 v] and wait: These powerful blocks allow different sprites to communicate with each other.[8] A sprite can broadcast a message, and other sprites that have a "when I receive [message]" block will then execute the attached scripts.[9] This enables complex interactions and coordinated behaviors between multiple elements.

Actions Triggered by Events:

Once an event occurs, you can trigger a variety of actions using blocks from different categories:

- Movement: As discussed earlier, events can trigger sprites to move, turn, or change their position.[10]
- Looks: Events can change a sprite's costume, show or hide it, or make it say or think something.[11]

- Sound: Events can initiate the playing of sounds or change the volume.[12]
- Control: Events can trigger loops, conditional statements, or even the creation of clones of sprites.
- Variables: Events can change the values of variables, which can then affect other aspects of the program.

Example: Creating an Interactive Button:
1. Add a sprite that looks like a button to your project.
2. Create the following script for the button sprite:
3. Code snippet

when this sprite clicked
   say [Clicked!] for 2 seconds
   broadcast [button_clicked]
   4.
   5.
   6. Add another sprite (e.g., a star).
   7. Create the following script for the star sprite:

8. Code snippet

```
when I receive [button_clicked]
    change size by 20
    wait 1 second
    change size by -20
```

9.

10. Now, when you click the button sprite, it will say "Clicked!" and also broadcast a message called "button_clicked." The star sprite, upon receiving this message, will briefly increase and then decrease in size. This demonstrates how an event (clicking the button) can trigger actions in multiple sprites through broadcasting.

3.5 Creating Simple Animations and Stories

Building on movement and interaction, you can start to create simple animations and tell stories using Scratch. This involves coordinating the actions, appearances, and sounds of multiple sprites over time and in response to events.

Creating Animations:

Animation in Scratch often involves:
- Changing Costumes: Sprites can have multiple costumes, which are different visual representations of the same character or object.[13] By quickly switching between costumes (using the next costume or switch costume to [ ] blocks within a loop), you can create the illusion of movement, like a character walking or a ball bouncing.
- Moving Sprites Gradually: Instead of large, sudden movements, using smaller move steps within a loop, possibly combined with short wait blocks, can create smoother animations.
- Rotating and Scaling: You can use the turn blocks and blocks in the Looks category to change the size of sprites

over time, creating effects like growing or shrinking.

- Using Glide: The glide block is particularly useful for creating smooth transitions and animated movements across the Stage.

Example: Animating a Flying Bird:
1. Add a bird sprite that has multiple wing flap costumes.
2. Create the following script for the bird:
3. Code snippet

```
when [green flag v] clicked
forever
    next costume
    move 10 steps
    if on edge, bounce
    wait 0.1 seconds
```

4.
5.

This script will continuously cycle through the bird's costumes, move it across the Stage, make it bounce off the edges, and introduce a short delay between each frame, creating a simple flying animation.[14]

Telling Stories:

Creating interactive stories in Scratch involves:

- Using Multiple Backdrops: You can add different backdrops to represent different scenes in your story and switch between them using the switch backdrop to [ ] block, often triggered by events.
- Coordinating Dialogue: Use the say [ ] for [ ] seconds and think [ ] for [ ] seconds blocks to make your characters speak and think, advancing the narrative.
- Triggering Events Based on User Interaction: Use when this sprite clicked or when key [ ] pressed events to allow the user to interact with the

story, making choices that affect the plot.

- Using Variables to Track Progress: You can use variables to keep track of the story's state, such as the current scene, the player's choices, or the completion of certain tasks.[15]
- Broadcasting and Receiving Messages: Use messages to coordinate actions between different characters and the changing backdrops as the story unfolds.

Example: A Simple Interactive Story:
1. Add two character sprites and a backdrop for a forest scene.
2. For the first character:
3. Code snippet

```
when [green flag v] clicked
say [Hello! I'm exploring the forest.] for 3
seconds
ask [Do you want to join me? (yes/no)] and
wait
```

```
if <(answer) = [yes]> then
    broadcast [join_adventure]
    say [Great! Let's go!] for 2 seconds
else
        say [Okay, maybe next time.] for 2
seconds
```

4.

5.

6. For the second character:

7. Code snippet

```
when I receive [join_adventure]
say [Hi! I'm ready!] for 2 seconds
move 20 steps
```

8.

9. In this simple example, the first character asks the user a question. Based on the answer, a message is broadcast, which triggers a response from the second character.[16]

By combining movement, interaction through events, and the creative use of costumes, backdrops, dialogue, and messages, you can create a wide range of engaging animations and interactive stories in visual programming environments like Scratch. These projects not only reinforce your understanding of fundamental programming concepts but also provide a fantastic outlet for your creativity and storytelling abilities. So, let your imagination soar and start making magic with blocks!

Part II:

Diving Deeper: Introduction to Text-Based Coding

CHAPTER 4

Your First Lines of Code: Introduction to Python

Having explored the visual and intuitive world of block-based programming, it's time to transition to a more traditional, yet equally powerful, way of communicating with computers: text-based coding. This chapter marks your first foray into writing code using characters, words, and specific grammatical rules. We'll introduce you to Python, a versatile and beginner-friendly programming language, and guide you through the initial steps of setting up your coding environment and writing your very first lines of code.

4.1 What is Text-Based Coding? Typing Your Instructions

While visual programming languages use graphical blocks to represent code, text-based coding involves writing instructions using a specific set of characters, words, and syntax (grammar) that the computer can understand. Instead of dragging and dropping blocks, you'll be typing out code in a text editor, similar to writing an essay or a poem.

Key Differences and Considerations:

- Syntax is Crucial: In text-based coding, syntax is paramount. Every character, word, and symbol must be in its correct place for the code to be interpreted correctly. Even a small typo or misplaced punctuation mark can cause errors and prevent your program from running.
- Greater Flexibility and Control: While visual programming offers a gentle introduction to coding concepts, text-based coding provides greater flexibility and control over the computer's behavior. You can express more complex logic and create more

sophisticated programs with text-based languages.

- A Stepping Stone to Professional Development: Most professional software development relies heavily on text-based coding languages. Learning a text-based language like Python is an essential step towards becoming a proficient programmer and opening doors to various career opportunities in the tech industry.

- Requires More Precision and Attention to Detail: Text-based coding demands a higher level of precision and attention to detail compared to visual programming. You'll need to be meticulous in your typing, pay close attention to syntax rules, and carefully review your code to identify and fix errors.

- Abstract Representation: Text-based code is more abstract than visual blocks. You'll need to develop the ability to visualize the flow of execution and the relationships between different parts of your code in your mind.

The Coding Process:

The general process of text-based coding involves the following steps:

1. Writing the Code: You'll use a text editor or an Integrated Development Environment (IDE) to write your code in a specific programming language.
2. Saving the Code: You'll save your code in a file with a specific extension (e.g., .py for Python files).
3. Running the Code: You'll use a program called an interpreter or a compiler to translate your code into a language that the computer can understand and execute.
4. Seeing the Output: The computer will execute your code and display the output, which could be text, numbers, images, or any other form of data,

depending on what your program is designed to do.

5. Debugging the Code: If your code contains errors (bugs), you'll need to identify and fix them. This process is called debugging and is a crucial part of the coding process.

4.2 Why Python? A Friendly First Language

When venturing into the world of text-based coding, choosing the right programming language to start with is essential. While many languages are available, Python stands out as an excellent choice for beginners due to its simplicity, readability, and versatility.

Reasons Why Python is a Great First Language:

- Easy-to-Read Syntax: Python's syntax is designed to be clear, concise, and similar to natural English. This makes it easier to understand and write code, especially for those new to programming. For example, to print something to the console, you simply use the print() function:

```
print("Hello, world!")
```

-
- This is much more straightforward than the equivalent code in some other languages.
- Large and Supportive Community: Python has a vast and active community of developers who contribute to its development, create helpful resources, and provide support to beginners. If you encounter a problem or have a question, you can easily find help online through forums, tutorials, and documentation.
- Versatile and Widely Used: Python is a general-purpose language, meaning it can be used for a wide variety of applications, from web development and data analysis to scientific computing and artificial intelligence.

This versatility means that the skills you learn with Python can be applied to many different projects and domains.

- Abundant Libraries and Frameworks: Python has a rich ecosystem of libraries and frameworks that provide pre-built tools and functions for various tasks. This allows you to write code more efficiently and avoid reinventing the wheel. For example, the NumPy library is used for numerical computations, Pandas for data manipulation, and Django and Flask for web development.

- Interactive Interpreter: Python provides an interactive interpreter, which allows you to execute code snippets and see the results immediately. This is a great way to experiment with the language, test out ideas, and learn by doing. You can type a line of code and see the output right away, without having to write an entire program.

- Focus on Readability: Python's design philosophy emphasizes code readability, making it easier to understand and maintain code written by yourself or others. This is crucial for collaboration and for writing code that is easy to debug and modify.
- Strong Educational Resources: Many excellent tutorials, courses, and books are specifically designed to teach Python to beginners. This makes it easier to find high-quality learning materials and progress at your own pace.
- Used by Industry Giants: Python is used by many prominent companies, including Google, Facebook, Amazon, and Netflix, for various purposes. This demonstrates its practicality and relevance in the real world and provides assurance that the skills you

learn will be valuable in the job market.

In essence, Python's combination of simplicity, readability, versatility, and a supportive community makes it an ideal language for your first foray into text-based coding. It allows you to focus on learning fundamental programming concepts without getting bogged down in complex syntax or arcane rules. As you progress, you'll find that Python's capabilities extend far beyond the basics, enabling you to create powerful and sophisticated applications.

4.3 Setting Up Your Python Environment

Before you can start writing Python code, you need to set up your development environment. This involves installing Python on your computer and choosing a code editor where you'll write your programs. Here's a step-by-step guide:

1. Install Python:
- Download: Go to the official Python website (python.org) and download the latest stable version of Python for your operating system (Windows, macOS, or Linux).
- Install: Run the installer and follow the on-screen instructions. Make sure to check the box that says "Add Python to PATH" during the installation. This will allow you to run Python from the command line.
- Verify Installation: Open a command prompt or terminal and type `python --version` or `python3 --version`. If Python is installed correctly, you should see the version number displayed.

2. Choose a Code Editor:

While you can write Python code in a simple text editor like Notepad, a dedicated code editor or Integrated Development Environment (IDE) provides features that make coding more efficient and enjoyable. Here are a few popular options:

- Visual Studio Code (VS Code): A free and highly customizable code editor with excellent support for Python (through an extension). It offers features like syntax highlighting, code completion, debugging tools, and more.
- PyCharm: A powerful IDE specifically designed for Python development. It provides a comprehensive set of tools for writing, testing, and debugging Python code. (Community Edition is free)
- Sublime Text: A lightweight and fast code editor with a clean interface and powerful features.
- Atom: A free and open-source code editor that is highly customizable.

For beginners, VS Code is a great choice due to its ease of use, extensive features, and free availability.

3. Set Up VS Code for Python (Optional, but Recommended):

If you choose to use VS Code, follow these additional steps:

- Install the Python Extension: Open VS Code, go to the Extensions view (Ctrl+Shift+X), search for "Python" by Microsoft, and install it. This extension provides enhanced Python support in VS Code.
- Select a Python Interpreter: In VS Code, press Ctrl+Shift+P to open the Command Palette, type "Python: Select Interpreter," and choose the Python installation you want to use.

4. Virtual Environments (Optional, but Recommended for Larger Projects):

As you start working on more complex Python projects, it's best practice to create virtual environments. A virtual environment is an isolated space for your project that allows you to manage dependencies (external libraries) separately from other projects. This prevents conflicts between different project requirements.

- Create a Virtual Environment: Open a terminal or command prompt, navigate to your project directory, and run the following command:

python -m venv venv

-

- This will create a new virtual environment in a folder named "venv" within your project directory.
- Activate the Virtual Environment: Before working on your project, you need to activate the virtual environment. The activation command varies depending on your operating system:
  - Windows: venv\Scripts\activate
  - macOS/Linux: source venv/bin/activate
- Deactivate the Virtual Environment: When you're finished working on your

project, you can deactivate the virtual environment by running the command deactivate.

4.4 Writing Your First Program: "Hello, World!"

Now that you have your Python environment set up, it's time to write your first Python program! The traditional first program in any programming language is the "Hello, world!" program, which simply prints the text "Hello, world!" to the console.

Here's how to write this program in Python:
1. Open a new file in your code editor (e.g., VS Code).
2. Type the following code:

```
print("Hello, world!")
```
3.
4. Save the file with a .py extension (e.g., hello.py).
5. Run the program:

- In VS Code: You can run the program by right-clicking in the editor and selecting "Run Python File in Terminal" or by pressing the Run button in the top right corner.
- From the command line: Open a terminal or command prompt, navigate to the directory where you saved the file, and type python hello.py (or python3 hello.py on some systems) and press Enter.

If everything is set up correctly, you should see the output "Hello, world!" printed to the console.

Congratulations! You've just written and run your first Python program. This might seem like a small step, but it's a significant milestone in your coding journey.

4.5 Understanding Basic Syntax: Commands and Structure

Now that you've written a simple program, let's take a closer look at the basic syntax of Python. Syntax refers to the set of rules that govern how code is written. Just like grammar in English, syntax in Python dictates how you structure your code to be understood by the computer.

Key Concepts:

- Commands (Statements): A command, also known as a statement, is an instruction that tells the computer to perform a specific action. In Python, a command is typically written on a single line. For example, the print("Hello, world!") line is a command that tells Python to display the text "Hello, world!" on the console.
- Functions: A function is a reusable block of code that performs a specific task. In Python, you call a function by writing its name followed by

parentheses (). The print() is an example of a built-in function that displays output. Some functions require arguments (data passed inside the parentheses), while others do not.

- Arguments: Arguments are the values or data that you pass to a function when you call it. In the "Hello, world!" program, the text "Hello, world!" is an argument passed to the print() function.

- Strings: A string is a sequence of characters enclosed in quotation marks (either single quotes ' ' or double quotes " "). Strings are used to represent text in Python.

- Variables: A variable is a named storage location in the computer's memory that can hold a value. You can assign a value to a variable using the assignment operator =. For example:

```
message = "Hello, world!"
print(message)
```

-
- In this case, the variable message stores the string "Hello, world!", and the print() function is used to display the value of the variable.
- Keywords: Keywords are reserved words that have a specific meaning in Python and cannot be used as variable names. Examples of keywords include if, else, for, while, def, class, and many more.
- Operators: Operators are symbols that perform specific operations on values or variables. Examples include arithmetic operators (+, -, *, /), comparison operators (==, !=, >, <), and logical operators (and, or, not).
- Indentation: Indentation refers to the spaces or tabs at the beginning of a line of code. In Python, indentation is crucial for defining the structure of your code and indicating blocks of code. For example, indentation is used to specify the code that belongs inside

a loop or a conditional statement. Consistent indentation is essential for writing correct Python code.

- Comments: Comments are notes that you add to your code to explain what it does. Python ignores comments when it runs the code. You can create a single-line comment using the # symbol:

```
# This is a comment
print("Hello, world!")   # This is another comment
```

-
- You can also create multi-line comments using triple quotes ''' ''' or """ """.

```
'''
This is a
multi-line comment
'''

print("Hello, world!")
```

-

Understanding these basic syntax concepts is crucial for writing correct and readable Python code. As you learn more about Python, you'll encounter more advanced syntax rules and structures, but mastering these fundamentals will provide a solid foundation for your programming journey.

CHAPTER 5

Working with Data: Numbers, Words, and Variables

In the realm of programming, data is the foundation upon which everything is built. Whether you're performing complex calculations, processing user input, or manipulating information, understanding how to work with different types of data is essential. Python, being a versatile and powerful language, provides robust support for handling various data types, including numbers and text. In this section, we'll explore these fundamental data types and how they are utilized in Python programming.

5.1 Numbers in Code: Integers and Floats

Numbers are a cornerstone of programming, and Python offers several built-in numeric types to represent and manipulate numerical data. The two most common ones are integers and floats.

Integers

Integers, often abbreviated as int, represent whole numbers without any fractional or decimal part. They can be positive, negative, or zero. Examples of integers include:

10, -5, 0, 1000, -200

In Python, you can perform various arithmetic operations on integers, such as addition, subtraction, multiplication, division, and more.

```
a = 10
b = 5

print(a + b)  # Output: 15
print(a - b)  # Output: 5
print(a * b)  # Output: 50
```

```python
print(a / b)  # Output: 2.0 (Note: division of
integers can result in a float in Python 3)
print(a // b) # Output: 2 (Floor division -
discards the fractional part)
print(a % b)  # Output: 0 (Modulo - returns
the remainder)
print(a ** b)  # Output: 100000
(Exponentiation - a raised to the power of b)
```

Floats

Floating-point numbers, or float, represent real numbers with a fractional part or a decimal point. They are used to approximate numbers that cannot be precisely represented as integers. Examples of floats include:

3.14, -2.5, 0.0, 10.0, -0.001

Similar to integers, you can perform arithmetic operations on floats. However, it's important to be aware that floating-point arithmetic can sometimes introduce small inaccuracies due to the way computers represent these numbers.

```
x = 3.14
y = 2.0

print(x + y)  # Output: 5.14
print(x - y)  # Output: 1.14
print(x * y)  # Output: 6.28
print(x / y)  # Output: 1.57
print(x ** y)  # Output: 9.8596
(Exponentiation)
```

Type Conversion

In Python, you can convert numbers from one type to another using built-in functions:

- int(): Converts a value to an integer. If you pass a float, it will truncate the decimal part.
- float(): Converts a value to a float.

```
a = 10
b = 3.14
```

```python
c = float(a)  # Convert integer to float
d = int(b)    # Convert float to integer

print(c)  # Output: 10.0
print(d)  # Output: 3
```

5.2 Text in Code: Strings and Characters

Text is another fundamental data type in programming, and Python provides robust support for handling textual data through strings.

Strings

A string, denoted as str, is a sequence of characters enclosed in either single quotes ('...') or double quotes ("..."). Strings can represent words, sentences, paragraphs, or any other sequence of characters. Examples of strings include:

"Hello, world!", 'Python programming', "12345", "This is a string."

Python offers a wide range of operations and methods for working with strings:

- Concatenation: You can combine strings using the + operator.

```python
str1 = "Hello, "
str2 = "world!"
result = str1 + str2
print(result)  # Output: Hello, world!
```

-
- String Formatting: You can insert values into strings using placeholders or formatting techniques.

```python
name = "Alice"
age = 30
message = "My name is {} and I am {} years old.".format(name, age)
print(message)  # Output: My name is Alice and I am 30 years old.
```

```
#Using f-strings (Python 3.6+)
message_f = f"My name is {name} and I am
{age} years old."
print(message_f)
```

-
- String Methods: Python provides
  numerous built-in methods for
  manipulating strings, such as:
  - len(): Returns the length of a
    string.
  - lower(): Converts a string to
    lowercase.
  - upper(): Converts a string to
    uppercase.
  - strip(): Removes leading and
    trailing whitespace.
  - split(): Splits a string into a list
    of substrings.
  - replace(): Replaces occurrences
    of a substring with another
    substring.
  - find(): Searches for a substring
    within a string.

```python
text = " Python Programming "

print(len(text))        # Output: 20
print(text.lower())         # Output:  python
programming
print(text.upper())     # Output:  PYTHON
PROGRAMMING
print(text.strip())         # Output: Python
Programming
print(text.split())         # Output: ['Python',
'Programming']
print(text.replace("Python", "Java"))    #
Output:  Java Programming
print(text.find("Programming")) # Output:
9
```

-

Characters

In Python, there isn't a separate data type specifically for single characters. Characters are simply represented as strings of length one. For example:

```python
char = 'A'
```

```
print(type(char)) # Output: <class 'str'>
print(len(char))  # Output: 1
```

You can access individual characters within a string using indexing, where the first character has an index of 0.

```
text = "Python"
first_char = text[0]   # Access the first character ('P')
second_char = text[1] # Access the second character ('y')
last_char = text[-1]   # Access the last character ('n')

print(first_char)  # Output: P
print(second_char) # Output: y
print(last_char)   # Output: n
```

Strings are immutable, meaning that once you create a string, you cannot change its individual characters. However, you can create new strings by modifying or combining existing ones.

Understanding how to work with numbers and strings is fundamental to programming in Python. These data types are used extensively in various programming tasks, from performing calculations and processing data to interacting with users and displaying information. By mastering these basic concepts, you'll be well-equipped to write more complex and sophisticated Python programs.

5.3 What are Variables? Storing Information

In programming, variables are like containers or labeled storage locations in the computer's memory. They allow you to store and manage data that can be used and manipulated throughout your program. Instead of directly working with raw data (like numbers or text), you can assign meaningful names to these values and refer to them using variables.

Think of it like this: Imagine you have a box labeled "age" to store someone's age, or a box labeled "name" to store their name. You can easily access and modify the data in these boxes without having to remember the actual values themselves.

Key Points:

- Variables are used to store data.
- Each variable has a unique name.
- Variables make your code more readable and organized.
- You can change the value stored in a variable.

5.4 Giving Variables Names and Assigning Values

In Python, you create a variable by choosing a name and assigning a value to it using the assignment operator =. The syntax is straightforward:

```
variable_name = value
```

- variable_name is the name you choose for the variable.
- value is the data you want to store in the variable.

Here are some examples:

```
age = 30
name = "Alice"
height = 1.75
is_student = True
```

In these examples:

- The variable age stores the integer value 30.
- The variable name stores the string value "Alice".
- The variable height stores the float value 1.75.
- The variable is_student stores the boolean value True.

Rules for Naming Variables

While you have some flexibility in choosing variable names, there are certain rules you need to follow:

1. Start with a letter or underscore: Variable names must begin with a letter (a-z, A-Z) or an underscore (_).
2. Can contain letters, numbers, and underscores: After the first character, variable names can include letters, numbers (0-9), and underscores.
3. Case-sensitive: Python is case-sensitive, so myVar, myvar, and MYVAR are considered different variables.
4. Cannot be keywords: You cannot use Python keywords (reserved words with special meanings) as variable names. Examples of keywords include if, else, for, while, def, class, and, or, not, etc.
5. Descriptive and meaningful: It's a good practice to choose variable names that are descriptive and convey

the purpose of the variable. This makes your code easier to understand.

Best Practices for Naming Variables

In addition to the rules, here are some best practices for naming variables:

- Use lowercase with underscores (snake_case): This is the most common convention in Python. For example: my_variable, user_name, total_count.
- Be concise but clear: Choose names that are short but still clearly indicate what the variable represents.
- Avoid single-character names (except for loop counters): Using names like x, y, or i can make your code harder to understand, except in simple cases like loop counters.
- Use meaningful abbreviations: If you need to abbreviate, do it in a way that is easily understandable (e.g., num_students instead of ns).

5.5 Basic Mathematical Operations in Python

Python provides a wide range of operators for performing mathematical calculations. You can use these operators with variables to manipulate numerical data.

Here are the basic arithmetic operators:

- Addition (+): Adds two values.
- Subtraction (-): Subtracts one value from another.
- Multiplication (*): Multiplies two values.
- Division (/): Divides one value by another.
- Floor Division (//): Divides one value by another and rounds the result down to the nearest integer.
- Modulo (%): Returns the remainder of a division.
- Exponentiation (**): Raises a value to the power of another.

Here are some examples of using these operators with variables:

```
a = 10
b = 5

sum_result = a + b          # Addition: sum_result is 15
difference_result = a - b   # Subtraction: difference_result is 5
product_result = a * b      # Multiplication: product_result is 50
division_result = a / b     # Division: division_result is 2.0
floor_division_result = a // b   # Floor Division: floor_division_result is 2
modulo_result = a % b       # Modulo: modulo_result is 0
exponentiation_result = a ** b   # Exponentiation: exponentiation_result is 100000

print("Sum:", sum_result)
print("Difference:", difference_result)
print("Product:", product_result)
```

```
print("Division:", division_result)
print("Floor                    Division:",
floor_division_result)
print("Modulo:", modulo_result)
print("Exponentiation:",
exponentiation_result)
```

You can also combine multiple operations and use parentheses to control the order of evaluation:

```
x = 2
y = 3
z = 4

result = (x + y) * z - x ** 2  # result is (2 + 3)
* 4 - 2 ** 2 = 5 * 4 - 4 = 20 - 4 = 16
print(result)  # Output: 16
```

By using variables and mathematical operators, you can perform calculations, manipulate data, and create dynamic and interactive programs in Python

CHAPTER 6

Making Choices and Repeating Actions in Python

In programming, you often need to make decisions based on certain conditions and repeat blocks of code multiple times. Python provides powerful control flow structures to handle these situations: conditional statements (if, elif, else) and loop statements (for and while).

6.1 Using if, elif, and else for Decisions

Conditional statements allow you to execute different code blocks depending on whether a condition is true or false.

The if Statement

The most basic conditional statement is the if statement. It has the following syntax:

```
if condition:
    # Code to execute if the condition is true
```

The condition is an expression that evaluates to either True or False. If the condition is True, the code block indented below the if statement is executed. Otherwise, the code block is skipped.

```
x = 10
if x > 5:
    print("x is greater than 5")  # Output: x is greater than 5
```

The else Statement

You can use the else statement to specify a code block that should be executed if the condition in the if statement is False:

```
if condition:
    # Code to execute if the condition is true
else:
    # Code to execute if the condition is false
```

```python
x = 3
if x > 5:
    print("x is greater than 5")
else:
    print("x is not greater than 5")  # Output:
x is not greater than 5
```

The elif Statement

When you need to check multiple conditions, you can use the elif (short for "else if") statement. It allows you to specify additional conditions to test if the previous if or elif conditions are False:

```
if condition1:
    # Code to execute if condition1 is true
elif condition2:
    # Code to execute if condition2 is true
elif condition3:
    # Code to execute if condition3 is true
...
else:
```

```python
    # Code to execute if none of the
conditions are true
```python
grade = 85
if grade >= 90:
    print("A")
elif grade >= 80:
    print("B")  # Output: B
elif grade >= 70:
    print("C")
else:
    print("D")
```

6.2 Repeating Code with for Loops

Loops allow you to execute a block of code repeatedly. The for loop is used to iterate over a sequence (such as a list, tuple, or string) or other iterable object.

for item in sequence:
    # Code to execute for each item in the sequence
```

```python
fruits = ["apple", "banana", "cherry"]
for fruit in fruits:
    print(fruit)
    # Output:
    # apple
    # banana
    # cherry
```

You can also use the range() function to generate a sequence of numbers to iterate over:

```
for i in range(5):  # Generates numbers from 0 to 4
    print(i)  # Output: 0 1 2 3 4

for i in range(2, 7):  # Generates numbers from 2 to 6
    print(i)  # Output: 2 3 4 5 6

for i in range(0, 10, 2):  # Generates even numbers from 0 to 8
    print(i)  # Output: 0 2 4 6 8
```

6.3 Repeating Code with while Loops

The while loop is used to repeatedly execute a block of code as long as a condition is True.

```
while condition:
    # Code to execute as long as the condition
is true
```

It's crucial to ensure that the condition eventually becomes False to avoid an infinite loop.

```
count = 0
while count < 3:
    print("Count:", count)
    count += 1
    # Output:
    # Count: 0
    # Count: 1
    # Count: 2
```

6.4 Combining Conditions and Loops for More Complex Tasks

You can combine conditional statements and loops to create more sophisticated control flow structures and handle complex tasks.

Combining if statements with Loops

You can use if statements inside loops to perform different actions based on conditions within each iteration:

```
numbers = [1, 2, 3, 4, 5, 6]
for number in numbers:
    if number % 2 == 0:
        print(number, "is even")
    else:
        print(number, "is odd")
    # Output:
    # 1 is odd
    # 2 is even
    # 3 is odd
    # 4 is even
    # 5 is odd
```

6 is even

Nested Loops

You can also nest loops inside other loops to iterate over multiple sequences or perform repetitive actions at multiple levels:

```python
for i in range(3):
  for j in range(2):
    print(f"({i}, {j})")
  # Output:
  # (0, 0)
  # (0, 1)
  # (1, 0)
  # (1, 1)
  # (2, 0)
  # (2, 1)
```

Loop Control Statements: break **and** continue

- break: Terminates the loop prematurely, and the program

execution continues with the statement after the loop.

- continue: Skips the rest of the current iteration and proceeds to the next iteration of the loop.

```
for number in numbers:
  if number == 4:
    break  # Exit the loop when number is 4
  print(number)  # Output: 1 2 3

for number in numbers:
  if number % 2 != 0:
    continue  # Skip odd numbers
  print(number)  # Output: 2 4 6
```

By effectively using conditional statements and loops, you can control the flow of your Python programs, make decisions, repeat actions, and handle a wide range of programming tasks.

Part III:

Building Your Own Apps!

CHAPTER 7

Introduction to App Development: What Makes an App?

Introduction to App Development: What Makes an App?
In today's digital age, apps have become an integral part of our daily lives. From social networking and entertainment to productivity and education, apps have transformed the way we interact with technology and the world around us. But what exactly is an app, and what goes into creating one?

7.1 What is an App? Exploring Different Types of Apps

An "app," short for "application," is a software program designed to perform a specific function or a set of related functions. Apps are primarily designed to run on mobile devices such as smartphones and tablets, but they can also run on desktop computers, web browsers, and even smart TVs.

Types of Apps

Apps can be broadly categorized into several types, depending on their purpose, functionality, and the technology used to build them:

- **Native Apps:** These are designed to run on a specific operating system, such as iOS (for Apple devices) or Android. Native apps are typically developed using platform-specific programming languages (e.g., Swift for iOS, Java or Kotlin for Android) and have full access to the device's hardware and features, resulting in high performance and a seamless user experience.
- **Web Apps:** These are accessed through a web browser, just like any other website. Web apps are built

using web technologies such as HTML, CSS, and JavaScript and can run on various platforms without requiring users to download or install anything. While they offer cross-platform compatibility, they may have limited access to device hardware and offline capabilities compared to native apps.

- **Hybrid Apps:** These combine elements of both native and web apps. They are built using web technologies but are wrapped in a native container, allowing them to be installed on mobile devices and access some device features. Frameworks like Apache Cordova and React Native enable developers to build hybrid apps using a single codebase, which can then be deployed on multiple platforms.
- **Progressive Web Apps (PWAs):** These are web applications that can function like native apps on mobile devices. PWAs offer features like

offline access, push notifications, and home screen installation, providing a more immersive user experience while still being accessible through a web browser.

7.2 Basic App Structure: Screens, Buttons, and More

Regardless of the type, most apps share a common structure comprising several key elements:

- **Screens (or Views):** These are the individual interfaces that users see when interacting with an app. An app can have multiple screens, each serving a specific purpose. For example, a social networking app might have screens for the news feed, user profiles, settings, and messaging.
- **Layout:** This refers to the arrangement of elements on a screen, such as text, images, and buttons. A well-designed layout ensures that the

app is visually appealing, easy to navigate, and provides a consistent user experience.

- **User Interface (UI) Elements:** These are the interactive components that users use to interact with the app. Common UI elements include:
  - **Buttons:** Allow users to perform actions, such as submitting a form, navigating to another screen, or triggering a specific function.
  - **Text Fields:** Enable users to enter text, such as usernames, passwords, or search queries.
  - **Labels:** Display static text to provide information or instructions to the user.
  - **Images:** Display visual content, such as photos, icons, or illustrations.
  - **Lists:** Display collections of data, such as contacts, products, or messages.

- ○ **Menus:** Provide a list of options or commands for the user to choose from.
- **Navigation:** This refers to how users move between different screens or sections of an app. Effective navigation is crucial for ensuring a smooth and intuitive user experience. Common navigation patterns include:
  - ○ **Bottom Navigation:** A menu at the bottom of the screen for accessing primary sections.
  - ○ **Top Navigation:** A bar at the top of the screen, often used for displaying the app title and navigation controls.
  - ○ **Drawer Navigation:** A hidden menu that slides in from the side of the screen.

7.3 Understanding User Interface (UI) and User Experience (UX)

In app development, UI and UX are two critical concepts that play a significant role in the success of an app:

- **User Interface (UI):** This refers to the visual elements and interactive components that users see and interact with. A well-designed UI should be visually appealing, consistent, and easy to use.
- **User Experience (UX):** This encompasses the overall experience that users have when interacting with an app. A positive UX is characterized by factors such as ease of use, efficiency, enjoyment, and satisfaction.

While UI focuses on the look and feel of an app, UX considers the user's entire journey, from initial interaction to long-term usage. Both UI and UX are essential for creating apps that are not only functional but also enjoyable and engaging to use.

7.4 Planning Your First App: Ideas and Simple Designs

Before diving into the technical aspects of app development, it's crucial to plan your app effectively. Here's a basic process to get you started:

1. **Brainstorm Ideas:** Start by brainstorming potential app ideas. Think about problems you want to solve, needs you want to address, or interests you want to explore. Consider your target audience and what they would find valuable or enjoyable.

2. **Define Your App's Purpose:** Clearly define the purpose of your app. What problem does it solve? What value does it provide to users? A clear purpose will help you stay focused and make informed decisions throughout the development process.

3. **Identify Core Features:** Determine the essential features that your app must have to fulfill its purpose. Focus on the core functionality and avoid adding unnecessary features that could clutter the app and confuse users.

4. **Sketch Simple Designs (Wireframes):** Create simple sketches or wireframes of your app's screens. Wireframes are basic visual representations of the app's layout and structure, without focusing on detailed design elements. They help you visualize the user flow, plan the placement of UI elements, and ensure that the app is easy to navigate.

5. **Gather Feedback:** Share your app idea and designs with potential users or mentors and gather feedback. This will help you validate your idea, identify potential issues, and refine your app concept before moving on to development.

- **Why Gather Feedback?**
  - **Validate Your Idea**: Feedback helps determine if there's a genuine need or desire for your app.
  - **Identify Potential Issues**: Users might spot usability problems or suggest improvements you hadn't considered.
  - **Refine Your Concept**: Feedback can guide you in making necessary adjustments to your app's features, design, and functionality.
  - **Save Time and Resources**: Catching issues early can prevent costly rework later in the development process.
- **Who to Ask for Feedback**
  - **Target Users**: The most valuable feedback comes

from people who are likely to use your app.

- **Peers and Colleagues**: Other developers or designers can provide technical insights and suggest improvements.
- **Mentors or Advisors**: Experienced individuals in the field can offer valuable guidance and perspective.
- **Friends and Family**: While not always your target audience, they can still provide initial reactions and identify potential usability issues.
- **How to Gather Feedback**
  - **Show Your Wireframes/Mockups**: Use visual representations of your app to help people understand your concept.

- **Ask Specific Questions**: Instead of asking "What do you think?", try questions like:
  - "Is the app's purpose clear?"
  - "Is the navigation intuitive?"
  - "Are any features confusing or unnecessary?"
  - "What features would you like to see added?"
- **Listen Actively**: Pay close attention to the feedback you receive, both positive and negative.
- **Be Open to Criticism**: Don't take negative feedback personally. Instead, see it as an opportunity to improve your app.

- **Use Surveys or Questionnaires**: For larger audiences, create structured surveys to gather feedback efficiently.
- **Conduct User Interviews**: For more in-depth feedback, conduct one-on-one interviews with potential users.
- **Create a Prototype**: If possible, build a basic interactive prototype to get more realistic feedback on the user experience.

CHAPTER 8

Building Simple Apps with Visual Tools (e.g., App Inventor)

Visual app development tools have revolutionized the way applications are created, making the process more accessible to a wider audience. Platforms like App Inventor, Scratch, and others, provide intuitive interfaces that allow users to build fully functional apps by dragging and dropping components, rather than writing complex code. This approach has opened up app development to educators, students, hobbyists, and even entrepreneurs with limited programming experience.

8.1 Exploring a Visual App Development Platform

A visual app development platform typically comprises several key components:

- **Design Interface:** A drag-and-drop interface where users can select and arrange UI elements.
- **Component Library:** A collection of pre-built UI components, such as buttons, text fields, images, maps, and sensors.
- **Logic Editor:** A visual programming environment where users can define the app's behavior using blocks or graphical representations of code.
- **Emulator/Testing Tool:** A tool for testing the app's functionality and appearance on virtual devices or real devices.

App Inventor

App Inventor, developed by MIT, is a prime example of a visual app development platform. It empowers users to create Android applications using a block-based programming language. The platform's intuitive design and comprehensive features make it an excellent tool for learning the fundamentals of app development and building practical applications.

Key Features of App Inventor

- **Drag-and-Drop Interface:** App Inventor's interface is divided into two main sections: the Designer and the Blocks Editor. In the Designer, users can drag and drop UI components from the Palette onto the Viewer to create the app's layout.
- **Component Palette:** The Palette contains a wide range of components, including:
    - **User Interface:** Buttons, labels, text boxes, sliders, switches, etc.
    - **Layout:** Horizontal and vertical arrangements, table arrangements.
    - **Media:** Images, audio players, video players, sound recorders, cameras.

- **Drawing and Animation:** Canvas for drawing, sprites for creating animations.
- **Sensors:** Accelerometer, gyroscope, location sensor, orientation sensor.
- **Connectivity:** Bluetooth, web, web sockets.
- **Storage:** File storage, TinyDB (a simple database).
- **Blocks Editor:** The Blocks Editor is where users define the app's behavior using visual programming blocks. These blocks represent code statements and can be snapped together to create event handlers, control structures, and functions.
- **Emulator and Companion App:** App Inventor provides an emulator for testing apps on a computer. Users can also download the MIT AI2 Companion app on their Android devices to test apps in real-time.

8.2 Designing Your App's Interface: Dragging and Dropping Components

The process of designing an app's interface in App Inventor involves the following steps:

1. **Open a New Project:** In App Inventor, start a new project and give it a descriptive name.

2. **Enter the Designer:** The Designer view is displayed by default when you create a new project.

3. **Select Components from the Palette:** Browse the Component Palette and choose the UI elements you want to include in your app's interface. For example, if you're creating a simple calculator app, you might need buttons for numbers and operations, and a label to display the results.

4. **Drag and Drop Components onto the Viewer:** Drag the selected

components from the Palette and drop them onto the Viewer, which represents the app's screen. You can arrange the components in a layout that suits your app's design.

5. **Customize Component Properties:** Each component has properties that you can modify in the Properties panel. These properties control the component's appearance and behavior. For example, you can change the text, font size, and background color of a button.

6. **Use Layout Components to Organize UI Elements:** Layout components, such as HorizontalArrangement, VerticalArrangement, and TableArrangement, help you organize and align UI elements on the screen. This ensures that your app's interface is well-structured and visually appealing.

7. **Add Functionality with the Blocks Editor:** Once you have designed the app's interface, you can switch to the Blocks Editor to define the app's behavior.

Example: Creating a Simple "Hello, World!" App

Let's create a basic "Hello, World!" app to illustrate the process of designing an app's interface in App Inventor:

1. **Open a New Project:** Create a new project in App Inventor and name it "HelloWorldApp."
2. **Enter the Designer:** You should be in the Designer view.
3. **Add a Button:** Drag a Button component from the Palette onto the Viewer.
4. **Add a Label:** Drag a Label component from the Palette onto the Viewer and place it below the button.
5. **Customize Button Properties:**

- In the Properties panel, change the Text property of the Button to "Click Me".
- Change the Font Size property to 20.

6. **Customize Label Properties:**
   - In the Properties panel, change the Text property of the Label to "Hello, World!".
   - Change the Text Color property to blue.
   - Change the Font Size property to 24.

7. **Arrange Components:** Use the alignment properties of the Screen or Layout components to center the button and label horizontally and vertically on the screen.

Once you have completed these steps, you have designed the user interface for a simple "Hello, World!" app. The next step would be to use the Blocks Editor to define the app's behavior, such as displaying a message when the button is clicked.

8.3 Adding Functionality with Blocks: Making Your App Work

In visual app development platforms, you typically add functionality using a visual programming language, often in the form of blocks that represent code statements.

App Inventor's Blocks Editor

App Inventor uses a Blocks Editor where you can drag and drop blocks to create event handlers, control structures, and functions.

- **Event Handlers:** These blocks define what happens when a specific event occurs, such as a button click, a screen touch, or a sensor reading. For example, the when Button1.Click block specifies the actions to be performed when Button1 is clicked.

- **Control Structures:** These blocks control the flow of execution in your app. Examples include:
  - if-else blocks for making decisions.
  - for and while loops for repeating actions.
- **Functions:** These blocks allow you to define reusable blocks of code that perform a specific task.
- **Variables:** These are used to store and manipulate data within your app.

Example: Adding Functionality to the "Hello, World!" App

In our "Hello, World!" app, we can add functionality to display a greeting when the button is clicked:

1. **Open the Blocks Editor:** In App Inventor, switch to the Blocks Editor by clicking on the "Blocks" button.
2. **Add a Button Click Event Handler:** Drag the when

Button1.Click block from the Button1 drawer in the Blocks palette.

3. **Add a Label Set Text Block:** Drag the set Label1.Text to block from the Label1 drawer and drop it inside the when Button1.Click block.

4. **Add a Text Block:** Drag a text block from the "Text" drawer and drop it into the socket of the set Label1.Text to block.

5. **Enter the Greeting:** Type "Hello, World!" in the text block.

Now, when the button is clicked, the app will change the text of the label to "Hello, World!".

Example: Creating a Simple Calculator App

Here's a more complex example of adding functionality to a simple calculator app:

1. Design the Interface:
   ○ Add a Label to display the input and result.

- Add buttons for numbers (0-9), operators (+, -, *, /), and control functions (C, =).
- Use Layout components to arrange the buttons in a grid.

2. Define Variables:
    - Create variables to store the first number, the second number, the operator, and the result.

3. Implement Event Handlers:
    - **Number Button Click:** When a number button is clicked, append the number to the Label's text.
    - **Operator Button Click:** When an operator button is clicked:
        - Store the current number in the first number variable.
        - Store the operator.
        - Clear the Label.
    - Equals Button Click:

- Store the current number in the second number variable.
- Perform the calculation based on the stored operator.
- Display the result in the Label.
  - **Clear Button Click:** Clear the Label and reset all variables.

8.4 Testing Your App on a Computer or Device

Testing is a critical part of the app development process. It allows you to identify and fix errors, ensure that your app works correctly, and verify that it provides a good user experience.

Testing on a Computer

App Inventor provides an emulator that allows you to test your app on your computer. The emulator simulates an

Android device and allows you to interact with your app as if it were running on a real phone or tablet.

Testing on a Device

For more accurate testing, it's essential to test your app on a real Android device. App Inventor provides the MIT AI2 Companion app, which allows you to connect your device to the App Inventor development environment and test your app in real-time over Wi-Fi or USB.

Testing Process
1. Connect to the Emulator or Device:
   ○ **Emulator:** In App Inventor, click on "Connect" and select "Emulator".
   ○ **Device:** Install the MIT AI2 Companion app on your Android device from the Google Play Store. Connect your device to the same Wi-Fi network as your computer, or use a USB

cable. In App Inventor, click on "Connect" and select "AI Companion". Then, either scan the QR code displayed in App Inventor with the Companion app or enter the connection code.

2. **Test the App:** Interact with your app, trigger different events, and test all the features and functionality.

3. **Debug and Fix Errors:** If you encounter any errors or unexpected behavior, use the debugging tools in App Inventor to identify the cause and fix the code.

4. **Iterate and Retest:** After making changes, retest your app to ensure that the changes have fixed the issues and haven't introduced any new problems.

Testing Tips
- **Test on Different Devices:** If possible, test your app on devices with

different screen sizes and Android versions to ensure compatibility.

- **Test in Different Conditions:** Test your app in various conditions, such as with different network connections (Wi-Fi, cellular), different orientations (portrait, landscape), and different input methods (touchscreen, keyboard).
- **Perform User Testing:** Ask other people to test your app and provide feedback. This can help you identify usability issues that you may have missed.

8.5 Sharing Your Creations with Friends and Family

Once you've built and tested your app, you'll probably want to share it with others. App Inventor provides several ways to share your creations:

1. Download the APK File

You can download the APK (Android Package Kit) file of your app, which can then be installed on any Android device.

- In App Inventor, click on "Build" and select "Android App (.apk)".
- App Inventor will compile your app and generate the APK file.
- Once the APK file is generated, you can download it to your computer.
- You can then share the APK file with others via email, messaging apps, or file-sharing services.
- To install the APK file on an Android device, you'll need to enable "Install unknown apps" in the device's security settings.

2. Share the AIA File
- You can share the project's AIA (App Inventor Archive) file, which contains the app's source code. This allows others to import the project into their own App Inventor environment and modify or build upon it.

- In App Inventor, click on "Project" and select "Export selected project (.aia) to my computer".
- The AIA file will be downloaded to your computer, and you can share it with others.
- In App Inventor, others can import the AIA file by clicking on "Project" and selecting "Import project (.aia) from my computer".

3. Publish to Google Play Store

To make your app available to a wider audience, you can publish it on the Google Play Store. This involves creating a developer account, providing app details (description, screenshots, etc.), and uploading the APK file.

Important Considerations When Sharing

- **User Privacy:** Be mindful of user privacy and ensure that your app complies with relevant privacy laws and guidelines, especially if it collects or processes personal data.
- **App Permissions:** Declare the permissions your app requires (e.g., access to camera, location, internet) and explain why they are needed.
- **Terms of Service and Copyright:** If your app uses any third-party libraries or resources, ensure that you comply with their terms of service and respect copyright laws.

CHAPTER 9

Introduction to Mobile App Development with Code (e.g., Python with Frameworks)

Introduction to Mobile App Development with Code (e.g., Python with Frameworks)
While visual app development tools like App Inventor have made app creation accessible to non-programmers, coding mobile apps with languages like Python offers greater flexibility, control, and the ability to create more complex and feature-rich applications.

9.1 Taking the Next Step: Coding Mobile Apps

Coding mobile apps involves writing instructions in a programming language that the device's operating system can understand. This approach provides several advantages:

- **Greater Control:** Developers have precise control over every aspect of the app's behavior and appearance.
- **Access to Native Features:** Coding allows you to utilize the full range of device capabilities, such as GPS, camera, sensors, and more.
- **Performance Optimization:** Coded apps can be optimized for performance, resulting in faster and more efficient applications.
- **Complex Functionality:** Coding enables the implementation of advanced features, such as complex data processing, custom animations, and seamless integration with web services.

9.2 Introduction to a Beginner-Friendly Mobile Development Framework

While native languages like Java (for Android) and Swift (for iOS) are commonly used for mobile development, frameworks like Kivy and BeeWare allow developers to use Python, a popular and beginner-friendly language, to create mobile apps.

Python for Mobile App Development

Python's simplicity, readability, and extensive libraries make it an excellent choice for learning to code mobile apps. Frameworks like Kivy and BeeWare abstract away some of the complexities of mobile development, allowing you to write Python code that can be deployed on multiple platforms, including Android and iOS.

Kivy

Kivy is an open-source Python framework for developing multi-touch applications. It allows you to write code once and deploy it on various platforms, including Android, iOS, Windows, macOS, and Linux. Kivy uses a custom UI toolkit and provides a wide range of widgets and tools for creating interactive and visually appealing apps.

BeeWare

BeeWare is a collection of tools that allows you to write native apps in Python and deploy them on multiple platforms. Unlike Kivy, which uses its own UI toolkit, BeeWare uses native UI elements, providing a more consistent user experience across different platforms.

9.3 Setting Up Your Development Environment for Mobile Apps

Before you can start coding mobile apps, you need to set up your development environment. This typically involves the following steps:

1. **Install Python:** If you don't have Python installed on your system, download and install the latest version from the official Python website (python.org).
2. **Install a Mobile Development Framework:** Install either Kivy or BeeWare, depending on your

preference. You can use pip, Python's package manager, to install these frameworks.

- **Kivy:** pip install kivy
- **BeeWare:** pip install beeware

3. **Install Dependencies:** Mobile development frameworks often require additional dependencies, such as libraries for handling graphics, audio, and other functionalities. Follow the framework's documentation to install any necessary dependencies.

4. **Set up Platform-Specific Tools:** Depending on the platforms you want to target (Android, iOS), you may need to install additional tools, such as:
   - **Android SDK:** For developing Android apps.
   - **Xcode:** For developing iOS apps.

5. **Choose a Code Editor:** Select a code editor or Integrated Development Environment (IDE) for

writing your code. Popular options include:

- **Visual Studio Code (VS Code):** A free and highly customizable code editor with excellent Python support.
- **PyCharm:** A powerful IDE specifically designed for Python development.
- **Sublime Text:** A lightweight and fast code editor with a wide range of features.

9.4 Creating Basic App Layouts with Code

Once you have set up your development environment, you can start creating your app's layout using code. Mobile development frameworks provide various layout components and widgets that you can arrange to create the desired user interface.

Kivy Layouts and Widgets

Kivy provides a variety of layout components, such as:

- **BoxLayout:** Arranges widgets in a horizontal or vertical box.
- **FloatLayout:** Allows you to position widgets at absolute coordinates.
- **GridLayout:** Arranges widgets in a grid.
- **StackLayout:** Arranges widgets in a stack.

Kivy also provides a rich set of widgets, such as:

- **Label:** Displays text.
- **Button:** A clickable button.
- **TextInput:** A text input field.
- **Image:** Displays an image.

Example: Creating a Simple Layout in Kivy

```
from kivy.app import App
from kivy.uix.boxlayout import BoxLayout
from kivy.uix.label import Label
```

```
from kivy.uix.button import Button

class MyLayoutApp(App):
    def build(self):
        # Create a BoxLayout
        layout = BoxLayout(orientation='vertical')

        # Create a Label
        label = Label(text="Hello, Kivy!", font_size=32)

        # Create a Button
        button = Button(text="Click Me", font_size=24)

        # Add the Label and Button to the Layout
        layout.add_widget(label)
        layout.add_widget(button)

        return layout

if __name__ == '__main__':
```

```
MyLayoutApp().run()
```

In this example, we create a vertical BoxLayout, add a Label and a Button to it, and display the layout in the app window.

9.5 Adding Simple Interactive Elements

To make your app interactive, you need to add functionality that responds to user input, such as button clicks, text input, and gestures. Mobile development frameworks provide mechanisms for handling events and updating the UI accordingly.

Kivy Event Handling

In Kivy, you can define event handlers for widgets using callbacks. For example, you can define a function that is called when a button is clicked.

Example: Handling a Button Click in Kivy

```
from kivy.app import App
```

```python
from kivy.uix.boxlayout import BoxLayout
from kivy.uix.label import Label
from kivy.uix.button import Button

class MyInteractiveApp(App):
    def build(self):
        # Create a BoxLayout
        layout = BoxLayout(orientation='vertical')
        self.label = Label(text="Click the button!", font_size=32)

        # Create a Button and attach a callback function
        button = Button(text="Click Me", font_size=24)

        button.bind(on_press=self.on_button_click)

        # Add the Label and Button to the Layout
        layout.add_widget(self.label)
        layout.add_widget(button)
```

```
        return layout

    def on_button_click(self, instance):
        # Update the Label's text when the
button is clicked
        self.label.text = "Button clicked!"

if __name__ == '__main__':
    MyInteractiveApp().run()
```

In this example, we define an on_button_click function that updates the Label's text when the button is clicked. We then use the button.bind() method to attach this function to the button's on_press event.

Part IV:

Leveling Up Your Coding Skills

CHAPTER 10

Working with Lists and Collections of Data

In programming, we often need to work with multiple pieces of information. Instead of creating individual variables for each item, we can use data structures to organize and manage collections of data efficiently. This section introduces you to lists, tuples, and dictionaries, and shows you how to use loops to iterate over them.

10.1 What are Lists? Organizing Multiple Pieces of Information

A list is a versatile and fundamental data structure that allows you to store an ordered collection of items. Lists are:

- Ordered: The items in a list have a specific order, and that order is preserved.

- Mutable: You can change the contents of a list by adding, removing, or modifying items.
- Heterogeneous: A list can contain items of different data types, such as numbers, strings, and even other lists.

Creating Lists

In Python, you create a list by enclosing a comma-separated sequence of items in square brackets [].

```python
# A list of integers
numbers = [1, 2, 3, 4, 5]

# A list of strings
fruits = ["apple", "banana", "orange"]

# A list of mixed data types
mixed_list = [1, "hello", 3.14, True]

# An empty list
empty_list = []
```

10.2 Accessing and Modifying Items in a List

Each item in a list has an associated index, which represents its position in the list. Python uses zero-based indexing, meaning the first item has an index of 0, the second item has an index of 1, and so on.

Accessing Items

You can access an item in a list using its index within square brackets.

```python
fruits = ["apple", "banana", "orange"]

# Access the first item (index 0)
print(fruits[0])  # Output: apple

# Access the third item (index 2)
print(fruits[2])  # Output: orange

# Access the last item using negative indexing
print(fruits[-1]) # Output: orange
```

Modifying Items

Because lists are mutable, you can change the value of an item at a specific index.

```
fruits = ["apple", "banana", "orange"]

# Change the second item (index 1)
fruits[1] = "pear"

print(fruits)   # Output: ["apple", "pear", "orange"]
```

List Methods

Lists provide several built-in methods for common operations:

- append(item): Adds an item to the end of the list.
- insert(index, item): Inserts an item at a specific index.
- remove(item): Removes the first occurrence of an item from the list.

- pop(index): Removes and returns the item at a specific index (or the last item if no index is provided).
- sort(): Sorts the list in ascending order.
- reverse(): Reverses the order of the items in the list.

```python
fruits = ["apple", "banana", "orange"]

fruits.append("grape")       # Add "grape" to the end
fruits.insert(1, "kiwi")     # Insert "kiwi" at index 1
fruits.remove("banana")             # Remove "banana"
removed_item = fruits.pop(0) # Remove and return "apple"
fruits.sort()                        # Sort the list alphabetically
fruits.reverse()             # Reverse the order of the list

print(fruits)
```

```python
print(removed_item)
```

10.3 Other Useful Data Structures: Tuples and Dictionaries (Introduction)

While lists are incredibly useful, Python offers other data structures with different characteristics:

Tuples

A tuple is similar to a list, but it is immutable, meaning you cannot change its contents after it is created. Tuples are defined using parentheses ().

```python
# A tuple of integers
numbers = (1, 2, 3, 4, 5)

# A tuple of strings
fruits = ("apple", "banana", "orange")
```

Tuples are often used to represent fixed collections of items, such as coordinates (x, y) or RGB colors (red, green, blue).

Dictionaries

A dictionary is a data structure that stores key-value pairs. Each key is associated with a specific value, and you can use the key to access the corresponding value. Dictionaries are defined using curly braces {}.

```
# A dictionary mapping fruit names to their colors
fruit_colors = {
    "apple": "red",
    "banana": "yellow",
    "orange": "orange"
}

# Access the color of a banana
print(fruit_colors["banana"])    #  Output: yellow

# Add a new key-value pair
```

```python
fruit_colors["grape"] = "purple"

# Modify the value associated with a key
fruit_colors["apple"] = "green"

# Remove a key-value pair
del fruit_colors["orange"]

print(fruit_colors)
```

Dictionaries are useful for representing data with labels or identifiers, such as configuration settings, database records, or mappings between words and their definitions.

10.4 Looping Through Lists and Collections

Looping allows you to iterate over the items in a list or other collection and perform the same operation on each item. Python provides the for loop for this purpose.

Looping Through a List

```
fruits = ["apple", "banana", "orange"]

# Iterate over each fruit in the list
for fruit in fruits:
    print(fruit)
```

Looping Through a List with Indices

If you need to access the index of each item while looping, you can use the enumerate() function.

```
fruits = ["apple", "banana", "orange"]

# Iterate over the list and get both the index
and value of each fruit
for index, fruit in enumerate(fruits):
    print(f"Index {index}: {fruit}")
```

Looping Through a Dictionary

When looping through a dictionary, you can iterate over the keys, the values, or both.

```python
fruit_colors = {
    "apple": "red",
    "banana": "yellow",
    "orange": "orange"
}

# Iterate over the keys
for fruit in fruit_colors:
    print(fruit)

#Iterate over the values
for color in fruit_colors.values():
    print(color)

# Iterate over both the keys and values
for fruit, color in fruit_colors.items():
    print(f"{fruit} is {color}")
```

List Comprehensions

List comprehensions provide a concise way to create new lists based on existing ones.

```python
numbers = [1, 2, 3, 4, 5]
```

```python
# Create a new list containing the square of
each number
squares = [number ** 2 for number in
numbers]

print(squares)  # Output: [1, 4, 9, 16, 25]

# Create a new list containing only the even
numbers
even_numbers = [number for number in
numbers if number % 2 == 0]

print(even_numbers)  # Output: [2, 4]
```

CHAPTER 11

Creating Your Own Tools: Introduction to Functions

As you begin to write more complex programs, you'll find yourself repeating certain sequences of code. Functions allow you to encapsulate these repeated code blocks into reusable units, making your code more organized, efficient, and easier to maintain.

11.1 What are Functions? Reusable Blocks of Code

A function is a named block of code that performs a specific task. Think of a function as a mini-program within your main program. It takes some input, processes it, and may produce some output.

Benefits of Using Functions

- Code Reusability: Functions allow you to execute the same code multiple times without rewriting it.
- Modularity: Functions break down complex programs into smaller, more manageable units.
- Organization: Functions improve code readability and make it easier to understand the program's logic.
- Abstraction: Functions hide the implementation details of a specific task, allowing you to focus on the bigger picture.

11.2 Defining Your Own Functions

In Python, you define a function using the def keyword, followed by the function name, a pair of parentheses (), and a colon :. The code block within the function is indented.

```
def greet():
    """This function prints a greeting message."""
```

```
print("Hello!")
```

- def: Keyword used to define a function.
- greet: Name of the function (should be descriptive).
- (): Parentheses that may contain parameters (input to the function).
- :: Colon indicating the start of the function's code block.
- """...""": Optional docstring that describes what the function does.
- print("Hello!"): Code block that performs the function's task.

11.3 Calling and Using Functions

To execute a function, you "call" it by writing its name followed by parentheses ().

```
greet()  # Call the greet function
```

When a function is called, the program's execution jumps to the function's code block, executes the statements within it, and then returns to the point where the function was called.

```
def greet():
  print("Hello!")

print("Start")
greet()  # Call the function
print("End")

# Output:
# Start
# Hello!
# End
```

11.4 Passing Information to Functions (Arguments)

Functions can accept input values called arguments. Arguments are passed to the function when it is called and are used within the function to perform its task.

Parameters and Arguments

- Parameters: Variables defined in the function definition that receive the input values.
- Arguments: Actual values passed to the function when it is called.

```python
def greet(name):
    """This function greets the person passed
in as a parameter."""
    print(f"Hello, {name}!")

greet("Alice")  # Call the function with the argument "Alice"
greet("Bob")    # Call the function with the argument "Bob"
```

In this example, the function greet() takes one parameter called name. When the function is called, the arguments "Alice" and "Bob" are passed to the function and assigned to the name parameter.

Multiple Arguments

Functions can take multiple arguments.

```python
def add(x, y):
    """This function returns the sum of x and y."""
    result = x + y
    return result

sum_result = add(5, 3)  # Call the function with arguments 5 and 3
print(sum_result)     # Output: 8
```

Default Argument Values

You can specify default values for parameters. If an argument is not provided when the function is called, the default value is used.

```python
def greet(name="World"):
    """This function greets the person passed in as a parameter.
    If no name is provided, it defaults to "World"."""
    print(f"Hello, {name}!")
```

```
greet("Alice")  # Output: Hello, Alice!
greet()        # Output: Hello, World!
```

This comprehensive guide has introduced you to the concept of functions, how to define them, how to call them, and how to pass information to them using arguments. Functions are essential building blocks for creating modular, reusable, and well-organized code. As you continue your programming journey, you'll find yourself using functions extensively.

CHAPTER 12

Making Your Programs More Interactive

Interactivity is a crucial aspect of modern software. Users expect to be able to interact with programs, provide input, and receive meaningful feedback. This section covers techniques for making your programs more interactive and robust.

12.1 Getting Input from the User

The input() function is Python's built-in tool for getting input from the user. It displays a prompt (optional) and waits for the user to enter text, which it then returns as a string.

```python
name = input("Enter your name: ")
print(f"Hello, {name}!")

age = input("Enter your age: ")
age = int(age)  # Convert the input string to an integer
```

```python
print(f"You will be {age + 1} next year.")
```

Key Points

- The input() function always returns a string, even if the user enters numbers. You need to convert the input to the appropriate data type (e.g., int(), float()) if you want to perform calculations or other type-specific operations.
- You can provide a prompt to the input() function to guide the user on what to enter.

12.2 Displaying Output in Different Ways

The print() function is Python's primary tool for displaying output to the console. It can take multiple arguments, which it separates by spaces by default.

```python
print("Hello,", name, "!")  # Output: Hello, Alice !
```

```python
print("The result is:", 10)   # Output: The
result is: 10
```

Formatting Output

Python offers several ways to format output
for better readability and presentation:
- f-strings (Formatted String Literals):
  A concise way to embed expressions
  inside strings.

```python
name = "Alice"
age = 30
print(f"Name: {name}, Age: {age}")   #
Output: Name: Alice, Age: 30
```
  -
  - The format() method: A versatile way
    to format strings with placeholders.

```python
print("Name:  {},  Age:  {}".format(name,
age))  # Output: Name: Alice, Age: 30
print("Name:  {1},  Age:  {0}".format(age,
name))  # Output: Name: Alice, Age: 30
```

```python
print("Name:       {name},       Age:
{age}".format(name="Alice",       age=30))
#using keywords
```
  -
  - String formatting with the % operator
    (older style):

```python
print("Name: %s, Age: %d" % (name, age))
# Output: Name: Alice, Age: 30
```
  -

Additional print() Options
  - sep: Specifies how to separate the
    arguments (default is a space).
  - end: Specifies what to print at the end
    (default is a newline character \n).

```python
print("a", "b", "c", sep="-")  # Output: a-b-c
print("Hello", end=" ")
print("World")  # Output: Hello World
```

12.3 Adding Graphics and Sound (Introduction)

While this section primarily focuses on text-based interaction, it's important to acknowledge that modern applications often involve graphical user interfaces (GUIs) and sound.

- Graphics: Libraries like pygame, Tkinter, and Kivy allow you to create windows, draw shapes, display images, and handle user interactions with graphical elements.
- Sound: Libraries like pygame and playsound enable you to play sound files, control volume, and even generate sound effects.

Diving into these libraries is beyond the scope of this introduction, but they are essential tools for creating engaging and immersive applications.

12.4 Handling Errors and Making Your Code More Robust

Error handling is crucial for creating reliable and user-friendly programs. Errors can occur due to various reasons, such as invalid user input, file not found, or network connection issues.

Exceptions

Python uses exceptions to represent errors. When an error occurs, Python raises an exception, which can disrupt the program's execution.

Try-Except Blocks

You can use try-except blocks to handle exceptions gracefully. The code that might raise an exception is placed in the try block, and the code that handles the exception is placed in the except block.

```
try:
    age = int(input("Enter your age: "))
```

```
    print(f"You will be {age + 1} next year.")
except ValueError:
    print("Invalid input. Please enter a valid
number for your age.")
```

In this example, if the user enters a non-numeric value, the int() function raises a ValueError exception. The except block catches this exception and displays an error message, preventing the program from crashing.

Multiple Except Blocks

You can have multiple except blocks to handle different types of exceptions.

```
try:
    file_name = input("Enter the file name: ")
    file = open(file_name, "r")
    content = file.read()
    print(content)
    file.close()
except FileNotFoundError:
```

```
    print(f"Error: File '{file_name}' not
found.")
except IOError:
    print("Error: An I/O error occurred while
reading the file.")
```

Finally Block

The finally block is executed regardless of
whether an exception occurs or not. It is
often used to clean up resources, such as
closing files or releasing network
connections.

```
file = None
try:
    file_name = input("Enter the file name: ")
    file = open(file_name, "r")
    content = file.read()
    print(content)
except FileNotFoundError:
        print(f"Error: File '{file_name}' not
found.")
finally:
```

```
    if file:
        file.close()   # Close the file if it was
opened
```

Raising Exceptions

You can also raise exceptions manually using the raise statement. This can be useful for enforcing constraints or handling specific error conditions in your code.

```
def get_age():
    age = int(input("Enter your age: "))
    if age < 0:
        raise ValueError("Age cannot be
negative.")
    return age

try:
    user_age = get_age()
    print(f"You are {user_age} years old.")
except ValueError as e:
    print(f"Error: {e}")
```

By implementing robust error handling, you can make your programs more resilient to unexpected input and runtime errors, improving the user experience and the overall reliability of your code.

Part V:

The Journey Continues

CHAPTER 13

Exploring Different Programming Languages and Paths

The world of programming is vast and diverse, offering a multitude of languages and career paths. This section provides a glimpse into some popular programming languages and explores exciting areas like web development, game development, and data science/AI.

13.1 A Glimpse into Other Popular Programming Languages

While you might already be familiar with some programming languages, here are a few more worth exploring:

- Java: A versatile, object-oriented language known for its platform independence ("Write once, run anywhere"). It's widely used in enterprise applications, Android development, and large-scale systems.

- C#: Developed by Microsoft, C# is a powerful language used for building Windows applications, web applications (using ASP.NET), and game development (using Unity).
- JavaScript: Primarily known as a client-side scripting language for web development, JavaScript is essential for creating interactive and dynamic web pages. With frameworks like Node.js, it can also be used for server-side development.
- PHP: A server-side scripting language widely used for web development. It's often used to create dynamic web pages and interact with databases.
- Swift: A modern and powerful language developed by Apple for building iOS, macOS, watchOS, and tvOS applications.

- Kotlin: A statically typed language that runs on the Java Virtual Machine (JVM). It's increasingly popular for Android development and can also be used for server-side development and web development.
- Go: A language developed by Google, known for its simplicity, efficiency, and concurrency. It's often used for system programming, network programming, and cloud-native development.
- Rust: A systems programming language focused on safety, performance, and memory management. It's gaining popularity for building reliable and high-performance applications.

13.2 Web Development: Building Websites

Web development is the process of creating websites and web applications. It involves a combination of different programming languages and technologies.

Front-End Development

Front-end development focuses on the client-side of a website, which is what users see and interact with in their web browser.

- HTML: The standard markup language for creating the structure of web pages.
- CSS: Used for styling web pages, controlling the layout, colors, fonts, and overall visual appearance.
- JavaScript: A scripting language that enables you to add interactivity and dynamic behavior to web pages.
- Frameworks and Libraries: Popular JavaScript frameworks and libraries like React, Angular, and Vue.js simplify the development of complex and interactive user interfaces.

Back-End Development

Back-end development focuses on the server-side of a website, which handles the logic, data storage, and server infrastructure.

- Server-Side Languages: Languages like Python, Java, PHP, Node.js, and Ruby are used to build the server-side of web applications.
- Databases: Databases like MySQL, PostgreSQL, MongoDB, and others are used to store and manage the data for a website.
- Frameworks: Frameworks like Django (Python), Spring (Java), Laravel (PHP), and Ruby on Rails provide tools and structures to streamline the development process.

Full-Stack Development

A full-stack developer is proficient in both front-end and back-end development, capable of building complete web applications.

13.3 Game Development: Creating Your Own Games

Game development is a creative and challenging field that involves designing, programming, and producing video games.

Game Engines

Game engines provide a framework and tools for game developers, including rendering, physics, audio, and scripting.

- Unity: A popular cross-platform game engine used for creating 2D and 3D games for various platforms. C# is the primary programming language used in Unity.
- Unreal Engine: Another powerful game engine known for its advanced graphics capabilities and used for creating high-quality games. C++ is the main programming language used in Unreal Engine.

Programming Languages

- C++: A fundamental language in game development, particularly for performance-intensive games.
- C#: Widely used in Unity for game scripting and logic.
- JavaScript: Can be used for creating browser-based games.
- Python: While not as common for high-performance games, Python can be used for game scripting, tools development, and creating simple games.

Game Development Roles

- Game Programmer: Responsible for writing the code that controls the game's behavior, mechanics, and features.
- Game Designer: Focuses on the gameplay, story, characters, and overall game experience.
- Game Artist: Creates the visual assets for the game, such as characters, environments, and animations.

- Sound Designer: Creates the audio elements of the game, including music, sound effects, and dialogue.

13.4 Data Science and Artificial Intelligence: The Future of Coding

Data science and artificial intelligence (AI) are rapidly growing fields that involve extracting knowledge and insights from data and creating intelligent systems.

Data Science

Data science involves collecting, processing, analyzing, and interpreting data to solve complex problems and make informed decisions.

- Python: A popular language in data science, with libraries like NumPy, pandas, scikit-learn, and Matplotlib for data manipulation, analysis, and visualization.

- R: A language specifically designed for statistical computing and data analysis.

Artificial Intelligence (AI)

AI involves creating computer systems that can perform tasks that typically require human intelligence, such as learning, problem-solving, and decision-making.

- Machine Learning (ML): A subset of AI that focuses on training algorithms to learn from data without explicit programming. Python is the dominant language for machine learning, with libraries like TensorFlow, PyTorch, and scikit-learn.
- Deep Learning: A subfield of machine learning that uses artificial neural networks with multiple layers to learn complex patterns from large amounts of data.
- Natural Language Processing (NLP): A field that focuses on enabling

computers to understand, interpret, and generate human language.

- Computer Vision: A field that enables computers to "see" and interpret visual information from images and videos.

Programming Languages and Tools

- Python: The most popular language for both data science and AI, thanks to its extensive libraries and frameworks.
- R: Commonly used for statistical analysis and visualization.
- Java and C++: Can be used for building high-performance AI applications.
- Specialized Tools and Frameworks: TensorFlow, PyTorch, scikit-learn, and others.

CHAPTER 14

Tips and Tricks for Becoming a Better Coder

Becoming a better coder is a journey that requires dedication, perseverance, and a passion for learning. Here are some valuable tips and tricks to help you on your path to coding excellence:

14.1 Practicing Regularly and Staying Curious

- Consistent Practice: The key to improving any skill, including coding, is consistent practice. Set aside dedicated time each day or week to write code, even if it's just for a short period.
- Coding Challenges: Websites like LeetCode, HackerRank, and CodeWars offer a variety of coding challenges and exercises to help you

sharpen your problem-solving skills and improve your coding abilities.

- Explore Different Languages: Don't limit yourself to just one programming language. Explore different languages to broaden your understanding of programming concepts and discover new ways to solve problems.
- Stay Curious: The world of technology is constantly evolving, so it's crucial to stay curious and keep learning. Follow blogs, attend webinars, and explore new tools and technologies to stay up-to-date.
- Personal Projects: Working on personal coding projects is a great way to apply your knowledge, experiment with new ideas, and build a portfolio of your work.

14.2 Learning from Mistakes and Debugging Your Code

- Embrace Mistakes: Mistakes are a natural part of the learning process.

Don't be afraid to make them, but more importantly, learn from them. Analyze your errors to understand why they occurred and how to avoid them in the future.

- Debugging Skills: Debugging is a crucial skill for any coder. Learn how to use debugging tools and techniques to identify and fix errors in your code. Practice reading error messages carefully and systematically tracing the flow of your program to pinpoint the source of the problem.

- Rubber Duck Debugging: A classic technique where you explain your code line by line to an inanimate object (like a rubber duck). This process can often help you identify logical errors or misunderstandings in your code.

- Code Reviews: Ask other coders to review your code and provide feedback. Code reviews can help you identify potential issues, improve your coding style, and learn from others' perspectives.

- Version Control: Use a version control system like Git to track changes to your code, revert to previous versions if necessary, and collaborate effectively with others.

14.3 Finding Resources and Communities for Young Coders

- Online Tutorials and Courses: Websites like Khan Academy, Codecademy, Coursera, and Udemy offer a wealth of free and paid coding tutorials and courses for all skill levels.
- Books: There are many excellent books available for young coders that cover various programming languages and concepts in an engaging and accessible way.
- Coding Communities: Online forums and communities like Stack Overflow, Reddit's r/learnprogramming, and Dev.to provide platforms for coders to

ask questions, share knowledge, and connect with others.

- Coding Clubs and Workshops: Look for local coding clubs or workshops where you can meet other young coders, work on projects together, and learn from experienced mentors.
- Open Source Contributions: Contributing to open-source projects is a great way to gain real-world experience, collaborate with other developers, and improve your coding skills.

14.4 Working on Projects and Building a Portfolio

In the realm of software development, merely possessing theoretical knowledge is insufficient. Employers and clients seek tangible proof of your capabilities. This is where working on projects and building a portfolio becomes paramount. This note delves into the significance of project-based learning and portfolio development, offering insights into best practices and strategies for creating a compelling showcase of your skills.

The Importance of Project-Based Learning

Project-based learning offers numerous advantages for aspiring and experienced developers:

- Practical Application of Knowledge: Projects bridge the gap between theory and practice, enabling you to apply concepts learned in real-world scenarios.
- Skill Development: Working on projects fosters the development of essential technical skills, such as programming, debugging, and problem-solving, as well as soft skills like communication, teamwork, and time management.
- Problem-Solving Abilities: Projects often present challenges that require you to think critically, analyze

problems, and devise effective solutions.

- Creativity and Innovation: Projects provide a platform for expressing your creativity and exploring innovative approaches to software development.
- Experience Building: Each project contributes to your overall experience, making you a more well-rounded and capable developer.

Building a Compelling Portfolio

A portfolio is a curated collection of your best projects, showcasing your skills, experience, and accomplishments. It serves as a powerful tool for demonstrating your abilities to potential employers, clients, or collaborators.

Key Components of a Strong Portfolio

- Diverse Projects: Include a variety of projects that demonstrate your proficiency in different programming languages, frameworks, and technologies. This showcases your versatility and adaptability.

- Project Descriptions: For each project, provide a detailed description that includes:
  - The project's purpose and objectives
  - The technologies used
  - Your role and contributions
  - Challenges faced and solutions implemented
  - The final outcome or result
- Visual Appeal: Design your portfolio to be visually appealing and easy to navigate. A clean and professional design enhances the user experience and reflects positively on your work.
- Code Accessibility: If possible, provide access to the source code of your projects through platforms like GitHub. This allows others to review your code and assess your coding style and practices.

- Live Demos: Include live demos or working examples of your projects whenever feasible. This enables viewers to interact with your creations and experience their functionality firsthand.
- Personal Branding: Infuse your portfolio with your personal brand by incorporating your logo, color scheme, and writing style. This helps you stand out and create a memorable impression.
- About Me Section: Include a concise and engaging "About Me" section that highlights your skills, experience, and career aspirations.
- Contact Information: Make it easy for potential employers or clients to contact you by providing clear and up-to-date contact information.

Types of Projects to Include

- Personal Projects: Projects you've undertaken out of personal interest or to explore new technologies.
- Academic Projects: Projects completed as part of your coursework or degree program.
- Freelance Projects: Projects you've worked on for clients on a freelance basis.
- Open-Source Contributions: Contributions you've made to open-source projects.
- Team Projects: Projects you've collaborated on with others, demonstrating your teamwork and communication skills.

Portfolio Presentation Platforms

- Personal Website: Creating your own website provides maximum control over the design and content of your portfolio.
- GitHub Pages: GitHub Pages allows you to host your portfolio directly

from your GitHub repository, making it ideal for showcasing code-focused projects.

- Online Portfolio Platforms: Platforms like Behance and Dribbble, while geared towards designers, can be adapted to showcase web development and other coding projects with a strong visual component.

Best Practices for Project Development

- Plan Your Projects: Before diving into code, take the time to plan your projects thoroughly. Define the scope, objectives, and features of your project, and create a detailed outline or wireframe.
- Version Control: Use a version control system like Git to track changes to your code, collaborate effectively with others, and manage different versions of your project.
- Write Clean Code: Adhere to coding best practices and style guides to write

code that is readable, maintainable, and efficient.

- Test Thoroughly: Test your projects rigorously to identify and fix bugs, ensuring they function as expected and meet the requirements.
- Document Your Code: Write clear and concise comments to explain your code and make it easier for others (and your future self) to understand.
- Seek Feedback: Don't hesitate to seek feedback on your projects from mentors, peers, or online communities. Constructive criticism can help you improve your skills and identify areas for growth.

By dedicating time and effort to working on projects and building a strong portfolio, you can effectively showcase your skills, demonstrate your passion for coding, and increase your chances of success in the software development industry.

CHAPTER 15

The Future is Yours: Keep Coding and Creating!

As you continue your coding journey, remember that you're not just learning a skill; you're unlocking a world of possibilities. The future is increasingly shaped by technology, and your ability to code empowers you to be a creator, innovator, and problem-solver in this exciting world.

15.1 The Power of Coding in the Real World

Coding is the language of the future, and its impact is already being felt across various industries and aspects of our lives:

- Artificial Intelligence (AI) and Machine Learning: Coding is at the heart of AI and machine learning, enabling computers to learn from data, make predictions, and automate tasks. From self-driving cars to virtual assistants, AI is transforming the way we live and work.

- Web and Mobile Applications: Coding is used to create the websites and mobile apps we use every day, connecting people, businesses, and information across the globe.

- Data Science: Coding skills are essential for data scientists who analyze and interpret complex datasets to extract valuable insights, driving decision-making in various fields.

- Game Development: Coding brings virtual worlds to life, allowing developers to create immersive and interactive gaming experiences.

- Virtual and Augmented Reality (VR/AR): Coding is used to develop VR/AR applications that create new ways to experience and interact with the world around us.

- Internet of Things (IoT): Coding connects everyday objects to the internet, enabling them to collect and exchange data, leading to smarter homes, cities, and industries.
- Healthcare: Coding is used to develop innovative healthcare solutions, such as electronic health records, telemedicine platforms, and medical devices.
- Finance: Coding powers the algorithms and systems used in online banking, trading, and financial analysis.
- Education: Coding is transforming education, with interactive learning platforms, educational games, and tools that personalize the learning experience.

15.2 Inspiring Stories of Young Coders

Many young coders are already making a significant impact on the world, demonstrating the power of coding to create positive change:

- Developing Apps for Social Good: Young coders have developed apps to address social issues, such as connecting homeless individuals with resources, promoting environmental awareness, and facilitating communication for people with disabilities.
- Creating Games for Education: Young game developers have created educational games that make learning fun and engaging, helping students master various subjects and develop essential skills.
- Building Websites for Nonprofits: Young coders have volunteered their skills to build websites for non-profit

organizations, helping them reach a wider audience and amplify their impact.

- Innovating New Technologies: Young coders have developed innovative technologies, such as assistive devices for people with disabilities, tools for sustainable living, and solutions for pressing global challenges.

These stories are just a glimpse of what's possible when young people learn to code. As you develop your coding skills, you too can use your creativity and knowledge to make a difference in the world.

15.3 What's Next? Continuing Your Coding Journey

As you continue your coding journey, here are some steps you can take to further enhance your skills and explore new opportunities:

- Specialize in a Specific Area: Consider focusing on a particular area of coding that interests you, such as web development, mobile app development, game development, data science, or AI.

- Learn Advanced Concepts: Dive deeper into computer science concepts, such as data structures, algorithms, software design patterns, and database management.
- Build Complex Projects: Challenge yourself by working on more complex projects that involve multiple programming languages, tools, and technologies.
- Collaborate with Others: Collaborate with other coders on projects, attend hackathons, and contribute to open-source projects to gain experience working in a team and learn from others.
- Seek Mentorship: Find a mentor who can provide guidance, support, and advice as you navigate your coding

journey and explore career opportunities.

- Stay Updated with the Latest Trends: The world of technology is constantly evolving, so it's essential to stay updated with the latest programming languages, frameworks, and tools.

15.4 Final Encouragement and Resources

Remember that learning to code is a journey, not a destination. Embrace the challenges, celebrate your successes, and never stop learning. Your ability to code empowers you to create, innovate, and shape the future.

Here are some additional resources to support you on your coding journey:

- Online Learning Platforms: Codecademy, Coursera, edX, Udacity, Khan Academy

- Coding Communities: Stack Overflow, Reddit (r/learnprogramming, r/coding), Dev.to
- Open Source Platforms: GitHub, GitLab
- Coding Challenges Websites: LeetCode, HackerRank, CodeWars
- Books: "Eloquent JavaScript" by Marijn Haverbeke, "Python Crash Course" by Eric Matthes, "Clean Code" by Robert C. Martin
- YouTube Channels: freeCodeCamp.org, The Net Ninja, Traversy Media

The future is yours to create. Keep coding, keep learning, and keep pushing the boundaries of what's possible.

Conclusion: Your Coding Superpowers Unleashed!

As you reach the end of this learning journey, it's time to celebrate how far you've come and look forward to the exciting path ahead. You've gained valuable knowledge and skills that will empower you to shape the future in meaningful ways.

A Recap of Your Coding Adventure

Throughout this journey, you've:

- Explored the fundamentals of coding and programming languages.
- Learned how to write code, solve problems, and create your own projects.
- Discovered the power of coding in various real-world applications.
- Been inspired by stories of young coders who are making a difference.
- Gained insights into how to continue your coding journey and explore new opportunities.

You've not only acquired technical skills but also developed crucial problem-solving, critical thinking, and creative abilities that will serve you well in all aspects of life.

Encouragement for Future Learning and Exploration

Your coding journey doesn't end here; it's just the beginning. The world of technology is vast and constantly evolving, offering endless opportunities for learning and exploration. As you move forward, remember to:

- Stay Curious: Keep exploring new programming languages, frameworks, and technologies.
- Embrace Challenges: Don't be afraid to tackle complex problems and push your coding skills to the limit.
- Collaborate with Others: Work with other coders, share your knowledge, and learn from different perspectives.
- Build and Create: Use your coding skills to bring your ideas to life and

create projects that inspire and make a difference.

- Never Stop Learning: Commit to lifelong learning and stay updated with the latest trends and advancements in the field of technology.

The Endless Possibilities of Code

Coding is more than just a skill; it's a superpower that empowers you to shape the world around you. With code, you can:

- Create Innovative Solutions: Develop cutting-edge applications, software, and systems that solve real-world problems and improve people's lives.
- Drive Technological Advancements: Contribute to the development of new technologies, such as artificial intelligence, virtual reality, and biotechnology, that are transforming industries and society.
- Express Your Creativity: Use code as a medium for artistic expression,

creating interactive art, digital music, and immersive experiences.

- Make a Positive Impact: Develop applications and tools that address social issues, promote sustainability, and empower communities.
- Shape Your Future: Coding skills are highly valued in today's job market and will continue to be in the future, opening doors to exciting and fulfilling career opportunities.

As you embark on your future endeavors, remember that you have the power to make a difference. Your coding skills, combined with your passion and creativity, can help you achieve your dreams and contribute to a better world.

Congratulations on completing this journey! Your coding superpowers have been unleashed. Now, go forth and create amazing things!

Appendix:

Appendix: Diving Deeper into Coding
This appendix provides additional information and resources to support your coding journey.

A. Glossary of Coding Terms

- Algorithm: A step-by-step procedure or set of rules for solving a problem.
- API (Application Programming Interface): A set of rules and specifications that allow different software applications to communicate with each other.
- Array: A data structure that stores a collection of elements of the same type in contiguous memory locations.
- Bug: An error or defect in a software program that causes it to behave unexpectedly.
- Class: A blueprint for creating objects in object-oriented programming,

defining their properties and behaviors.

- Code: Instructions written in a programming language that a computer can understand and execute.
- Compiler: A program that translates source code written in a high-level programming language into machine code that a computer can execute.
- Conditional Statement: A programming construct that performs different actions based on whether a condition is true or false (e.g., if-else statements).
- Data Structure: A way of organizing and storing data in a computer so that it can be accessed and manipulated efficiently.
- Debugging: The process of identifying and fixing errors (bugs) in a computer program.
- Function: A reusable block of code that performs a specific task.

- HTML (Hypertext Markup Language): The standard markup language for creating web pages.
- IDE (Integrated Development Environment): A software application that provides comprehensive tools for writing, testing, and debugging code.
- Iteration: The process of repeatedly executing a set of instructions (e.g., in a loop).
- JSON (JavaScript Object Notation): A lightweight data-interchange format that is easy for humans to read and write and for machines to parse and generate.
- Library: A collection of pre-written code that can be reused in different programs.
- Loop: A programming construct that allows a sequence of instructions to be executed repeatedly until a certain condition is met (e.g., for loop, while loop).

- Object: An instance of a class, representing a specific entity in a program.
- Object-Oriented Programming (OOP): A programming paradigm that organizes code around objects, emphasizing concepts like encapsulation, inheritance, and polymorphism.
- Parameter: A value that is passed to a function when it is called.
- Syntax: The set of rules that define the structure and grammar of a programming language.
- Variable: A named storage location in a computer's memory that can hold a value.

B. Useful Resources and Websites for Young Coders

- Code.org: Offers a wide range of coding tutorials and resources for all ages, including the popular "Hour of Code" initiative.

- Scratch: A visual programming language developed by MIT, allowing users to create interactive stories, games, and animations.
- Tynker: A platform that teaches coding through game-based learning, with courses for various skill levels.
- Khan Academy: Provides free coding courses in languages like JavaScript, HTML, CSS, and SQL.
- freeCodeCamp: A non-profit organization that offers free coding courses and certifications, along with a supportive community.
- ** ইয়ুথ কোডিং সোর্স (Youth Coding Source):** This is a free online platform in Bengali for young students.
- W3Schools: A website with tutorials and references for web development languages like HTML, CSS, and JavaScript.

C. Example Code Snippets and Projects

Here are a few example code snippets and project ideas to help you get started:

Example 1: A Simple "Hello, World!" Program in Python

```python
print("Hello, World!")
```

This code will print the text "Hello, World!" to the console.

Example 2: A Basic HTML Web Page

```html
<!DOCTYPE html>
<html>
<head>
  <title>My First Web Page</title>
</head>
<body>
  <h1>Welcome to My Website!</h1>
    <p>This is my first web page using HTML.</p>
</body>
```

```
</html>
```

This code will create a simple web page with a heading and a paragraph.

Project Idea 1: A Simple Calculator

Create a program that can perform basic arithmetic operations (addition, subtraction, multiplication, division) based on user input.

Project Idea 2: A To-Do List Application

Build a program that allows users to add, remove, and view items on a to-do list.

Project Idea 3: A Simple Game

Create a simple game, such as a guessing game or a rock-paper-scissors game, using a programming language of your choice.

D. Troubleshooting Common Coding Errors

- Syntax Errors: These occur when you violate the rules of a programming language's syntax (e.g., misspelling a keyword, missing a semicolon). The interpreter or compiler will usually provide an error message indicating the location and type of error.

- Logical Errors: These occur when your code doesn't produce the expected output, even though it doesn't produce any syntax errors. Logical errors are often caused by incorrect logic or algorithms.

- Runtime Errors: These occur while your program is running (e.g., dividing by zero, accessing an invalid memory location). Runtime errors can cause your program to crash or behave unpredictably.

Tips for Troubleshooting:

- Read the Error Message: If you encounter an error, carefully read the error message provided by the interpreter or compiler. It often contains valuable information about the cause and location of the error.

- Use a Debugger: A debugger is a tool that allows you to step through your code line by line, inspect variables, and identify the source of errors.
- Print Statements: Use print statements to display the values of variables and trace the execution flow of your program. This can help you pinpoint where things are going wrong.
- Break Down the Problem: If you're stuck on a complex problem, try breaking it down into smaller, more manageable parts.
- Search Online: Use search engines and coding forums to find solutions to common coding problems.
- Ask for Help: Don't hesitate to ask for help from teachers, mentors, or online communities.

E. Further Learning Paths and Languages

As you progress in your coding journey, you can explore various learning paths and programming languages, depending on your interests and goals:

- Web Development:
    - Front-End: HTML, CSS, JavaScript, React, Angular, Vue.js
    - Back-End: Python (Django, Flask), Node.js, Ruby on Rails, PHP
- Mobile App Development:
    - Android: Java, Kotlin
    - iOS: Swift
    - Cross-Platform: React Native, Flutter
- Game Development:
    - C++, C#, Unity, Unreal Engine
- Data Science and Machine Learning:
    - Python, R
- Desktop Application Development:

○ Java, C#, Python (Tkinter, PyQt)

This is just a small sample of the many programming languages and learning paths available. The best way to choose a language or path is to explore your interests, consider your goals, and try out different options.